RELATIONSHIPS:
EVERYTHING YOU NEED TO KNOW BEFORE GETTING MARRIED

DR WILLIAM SMALL

FIRSTWORLD PUBLISHING
DALLAS, TX

Relationships: Everything You Need to Know Before Getting Married
Copyright © 2020 Dr William C. Small
All rights reserved under international copyright law.

FirstWorld Publishing
5000 Eldorado Parkway, Suite 150-191
Frisco, TX 75033
www.drwillspeaking.com

Contents may not be reproduced in whole or in part in any form or by any means whatsoever, whether electronic or mechanical (including information storage, recording, and retrieval systems) without express written consent from the publisher.

ISBN – 13: 978-0-9972067-6-0
ISBN – 10:   0-9972067-6-4

Cover Photo: ©Istockphoto.com
Interior & cover design: FirstWorld Publishing

Unless otherwise indicated, all scripture quotations are from the King James Version of the Bible.

Scriptures were taken from the Thompson Chain-Reference Bible, Fifth Improved Edition, copyright © 1908, 1917, 1929, 1934, 1957, 1964, 1982, by Frank Charles Thompson.

All information contained in [ ] within verses of scripture was added by the author.

Hebrew and Greek definitions were taken from Strong's New Exhaustive Concordance Of The Bible, copyright © 1890, by James Strong, STD, LL.D. and cross referenced with Young's Analytical Concordance To The Bible, copyright © 1982, by Thomas Nelson, Inc.

Historical references were taken from Nelson's Illustrated Encyclopedia of Bible Facts, copyright © 1980 1995, by Thomas Nelson Publishers.

Visit WealthBuilderSeminars.com and Amazon.com for other books by Dr. William Small.

Relationships

Contents

DEDICATION	9
INTRODUCTION	13
Chapter 1	21
THE FIVE LEVELS OF RELATIONSHIPS	
Chapter 2	41
THE ESSENTIAL ELEMENTS OF LOVE	
Chapter 3	73
LOVE BUILDING BASICS	
Chapter 4	89
PREPARE TO CHANGE	
Chapter 5	119
FORGIVE AND LIVE	
Chapter 6	139
MEN vs. WOMEN	
Chapter 7	175
BOYS SHOULD PLAY WITH DOLLS	

Chapter 8 — 201
WHY IS IT HARD TO FIND LOVE?

Chapter 9 — 223
AVOID ATTRACTING ABUSIVE MEN

Chapter 10 — 239
HOW TO FIND A FAITHFUL MAN

Chapter 11 — 281
HOW TO FIND A VIRTUOUS WOMAN

Chapter 12 — 293
LOVE'S FINANICAL RISKS AND REWARDS

ABOUT THE AUTHOR — 313

RECOMMENDED READING — 315

DEDICATION

This book is dedicated to my beloved daughter, **Deandra,** and her generation.

Relationships

"Infantile love follows the principle: I love because I am loved. Mature love follows the principle: I am loved because I love. Immature love says: I love you because I need you. Mature love says: I need you because I love you."

~ *Erich Fromm*

Relationships

INTRODUCTION

The US Census Bureau reports that 53% of marriages in America end in divorce. And 60% of men and 55% of women have reportedly cheated or had extramarital affairs. According to the Canadian Department of Justice their divorce rate is about 48%. First marriages have a 50% chance of ending in divorce and the risk becomes greater with each successive marriage. The Canadian rate of divorce rises to 72% for second and around 85% for third marriages. In Australia, 40% of marriages are expected to end in divorce. Cohabitation before marriage in that country increased from 18% in 1975 to 60% today. The United Kingdom's Office of National Statistics reports that divorce rates in the UK have fallen over the last 5 years to 43%. This is largely due to fewer people getting married resulting in fewer divorces statistically. The leading causes of divorce in the UK are adultery and domestic abuse. Relationships: Everything You Need to Know Before Getting Married provides information that will help couples, regardless of country, build and maintain a happy and healthy relationship.

The level of heartache and heartbreak leading to divorce has grown to epidemic proportions worldwide. The failure of marital and co-habitation relationships does not just affect the mental health of the adults involved, it also impacts the psychological well being of their children. Most people who fail in marriage do not fail because of what they know.

They fail because of what they don't know. Not knowing how to be married after getting married causes a couple to need emergency assistance in learning how to build and maintain a happy and healthy marriage.

Everyone needs assistance periodically to help resolve emergency situations that arise in their relationships. As we visualized our relationship initially we thought it would always be happy. However, emergencies occur in relationships naturally because no one ever taught most of us exactly how to love and live with another person. We never learned the essential elements of love, love building basics or loves' financial risk and rewards. Lacking knowledge on how to build and maintain relationships leads to emotional trauma, communication glitches, fights, and financial problems. We enter into marital and co-habitation relationships without actually knowing what to do, therefore, we quickly find ourselves in immediate need of information that has the power to eliminate present and prevent future relationship emergencies.

Many couples have had to deal with heartache and headache in their marriage for so long that they think these maladies are a normal part of male/female relationships. In this book you will find insight on how to make happiness a normal occurrence in your relationship and make headache and heartache a thing of the past. You will discover the keys to being happy as well as the principles on how a couple working together can become wealthy! Your partner can be your passport to prosperity or the pathway to prolific profits. Choosing the right person can also improve your chances of reaching your professional goals. Two working together will always achieve more than one working alone.

Real people with real relationship problems and challenges need real answers to real questions. This book will attempt to address many of those pressing issues. It provides candid advice of which you will not always agree and in some cases may make you angry. The reason anger may arise in some is because what they will be reading is unadulterated truth. We live in an age where truth is controversial. While the truth may be controversial it is always incontrovertible. That is, one cannot stop it from being true no matter how angry it may make them or how distasteful it may be. Therefore, if you simply apply the truth in a way that makes sense for your life, it will assist you in building happy, loving, problem free relationships.

A study headed by Professor Kathleen Hutchinson "Talking to Daddy's Little Girl About Sex: Daughters' Reports of Sexual Communication and Support From Fathers" published in the Journal of Family Issues concluded that having intercourse later in life and fewer sexual partners is very good for a girl's sexual and mental

Relationships

health. These factors are influenced by girls maintaining open communication with their dads. This book contains knowledge that fathers can share with their daughters when they are having conversations about boys, love, and dating.

More often than not when people are experiencing relationship problems they tend to focus on what their partner is or is not doing. Having a happy relationship requires honesty which means looking honestly at both sides of whatever the issue is including what we may or may not be doing to contribute to the problem. Sometimes our partner may do something that we don't like but in order to keep peace or prevent an argument we don't say anything. That is, until we just can't take it anymore and then we blow up. Now our partner is confused because they did the same thing so many times before and we said nothing but all of a sudden there is a big problem. In relationships we love to assign blame so who is wrong here?

Our partner is wrong for doing whatever they did but we are also wrong for not correcting their behavior the first time it occurred. An explosive confrontation may be warranted if your partner was told about the effect of their behavior on you several times but they didn't stop. Usually, someone who cares for us will stop. However if we never tell them they will just keep doing what they were doing because they won't know that we have a problem with their behavior. The point is our partner's actions may be wrong, but we can cause a bigger problem by not addressing their behavior the first time it bothered us.

We will address some of the things that our partners may do and why. But we will also candidly discuss some of the things that we either do or allow that make our partners think that they can do what they do. It always takes two to tango and it takes two to argue.
One person can get beat up by another but it takes two to have a fight. One of the objectives of this book is to reduce or prevent fights and arguments in relationships. We will focus primarily, therefore, on providing knowledge and information that will lead to better understanding, provoke conversation, prevent arguments, and improve relationships. The more couples know about how to build a great relationship the quicker they can grow from contentious competitors to complementary companions.

In math, a "problem" is created when one side of an equation is out of balance with the other. The word "equation" means the process of seeking equality. Problems arise in a relationship when there is something on one side that creates inequality and the process of bringing it back into balance is not followed properly. Without equality in a relationship there is always going to be a problem. That problem will create contention which will keep the couple from being happy and having love. We must always look at both sides of the equation equally when there is a problem and the relationship has gotten out of balance. The goal however is not to assign blame but rather to recognize which side needs to have something added or subtracted in order for the couple to come into equality again or back into balance.

Achieving balance or equality is going to require change on one side of the equation. It is easy for a person to recognize the changes that others need to make.

The hardest thing for a person to do is to first recognize that THEY need to change and second to make that change. Change and/or resistance to change are the main factors that produce a lingering problem which leads to relationship failure. Rather than recognizing the need for and executing the requisite change, the person who really needs to change tries to force the other person to change. Sometimes they both try to force each other to change in every situation. However, if both sides changed in every situation the problem may never be solved because fluctuation, imbalance, and inequality would be present constantly. More often than not, one side must remain static and the other side must make the change necessary to bring balance or equality to the equation. It is important, though, to always examine both sides of the problem initially to see which side should remain constant and which side must make adjustments. Then, we can apply the proper formula to solve the problem, create balance, and achieve equality.

Equality is one of the essential elements of love. Without equality, a relationship cannot grow to the level of love. We will explore various methods that people can try to bring balance to their relationships, create harmony and symphony, and ultimately learn to be equally happy in love.

Whenever we have a problem with a product, if we want to solve that problem, we must either consult the manufacturer or read the manufacturer's operating instructions to understand how to fix it. People and relationships are products created by GOD.

GOD left us a book of operating instructions that provides knowledge on how to prevent and repair any problem we may have with people or relationships. Therefore, I will present some of the knowledge necessary for improving our relationships using references from the Bible. The Bible is the manufacturer's operating instructions for our life and relationships.

There are only three things that the Bible teaches: how to get along with GOD, how to get along with myself, and how to get along with others. It just teaches those three things many different ways. Teaching is repeating until learning takes place. You will find a few points or themes repeated throughout this book (e.g., feminine power, sexual virtue, and infidelity or cheating) because they are important issues that we must understand completely in order to build relationships that last long and remain strong as well as happy and healthy.

At the end of the day, every relationship must benefit two people mutually. Each person must be able to get what they need from a relationship or it will eventually dissolve. They key to longevity, then, if you love a person and you want your marriage to survive, is to make sure you understand what your partner needs and be sure they are getting it. Real love requires selfless service; in sickness and in health, for richer or poorer, until death do you part.

Chapter 1
THE FIVE LEVELS OF RELATIONSHIPS

"There is nothing nobler or more admirable than when two people who see eye to eye keep house as man and wife, confounding their enemies and delighting their friends."

~ Homer

The five levels of relationship are believe, faith, know, love, and trust.

Believe is the lowest level of relationship. This is the early stage in a relationship where we don't really know the person but we really like them. So we believe that we might be able to have a good relationship with this person.

We move to the faith level of a relationship once we can confess, without wavering, the belief that we can share a lifetime commitment to this person that we really like. This type of faith is an expression of a sincere hope that the marriage or relationship we have always dreamed of can come true. Moreover, the faith level of relationship is where we develop the hope of that which we fully expect to receive and we become happy in the anticipation of having a good relationship with the one that we like. We actually have no evidence to support our faith at this time.

Relationships

We just hope that we are right.

After spending time with and talking to the person that we like, we begin to move from faith to knowing that a relationship with this person will be good. The knowing or knowledge level of a relationship is achieved through intimacy. Contrary to popular belief intimacy comes through conversation not intercourse. Marriages often break down before they begin because couples spend too much time in intercourse and very little time engaged in the type of conversation that leads to intimacy. Two people become intimate when they reach that private space of vulnerability within each other's hearts and minds where they can clearly recognize the morals and values that shape their potential mate's character and integrity.

The purpose of intimate conversation is to create conversion or to bring two people to the point where they can see themselves becoming one. Conversation allows the couple to obtain intimate knowledge of each other and enable them to clearly see who the person is they will be committed to once they do get married and become one. Not having this level of intimate knowledge is what leads one or both of them to get cold feet at the wedding. At the time of ceremonial union they suddenly realize that they don't really know the person who they are about to make a lifetime commitment to.

Ladies, it is critical that you understand this clearly

when it comes to men and intimacy. Sex is considered an intimate act but it does not lead to intimate access of a man's mind.

Once he has gotten what he wants there is no incentive for him to give you what you need. There is no reason for a man to give you intimate access to the private place within his mind once you have sex unless he wants more sex. It is unproductive, then, to share physical intimacy with a man before receiving spiritual, mental, and emotional intimacy. Women have sex with a man hoping it will lead to lasting love. However, intimacy is the path that leads to love. Sex is not the path that leads to love. Sex (if it is good) is the path that leads to more sex. If a woman wants love, she has to refrain from engaging in sex until she achieves true intimacy. That is, if she is looking for lasting love and a marriage commitment.

Love for a man begins in his head not his heart. When you ask a man if he loves you, he has to think about it for a minute. If you ask him his opinion on a matter he will say "Well, I feel…" Feeling for a man is a matter of the mind not of the heart. There is another chapter in this book where I present the essential elements of love so I won't go into detail here. Just be aware for now that love does not start in a man's heart, it begins in his mind. The emotional center or heart of a man is not located in the center of his body it is in the center of his head. Therefore, if a woman wants to get to a man's heart, she has to get into his head. Most women instinctively know this which is the reason why you ask that question that most men hate: "Whatcha thinkin?" Notice also ladies, it is much easier for you to get an answer to that question before you have had sex with the man than afterward.

In order to have a long lasting relationship it must move or grow up to the fifth level of relationship which is trust. Trust begins with a belief that we can have a good relationship and moves to faith. Faith becomes knowing after we have obtained intimacy which leads to love. Love when applied equally, freely, and justly will lead to trust. Trust is the highest level of relationship where a couple can be open and naked before one another emotionally and have no doubt that their mate will not use their vulnerability against them. No matter what hardships they must endure to be and remain married, a couple will resolve to endure when they trust that they can reach their destination together. A relationship should have already reached the level of trust before a couple gets married. Otherwise once the trials and hardships of becoming married kick-in after they get married, it will be difficult for them to remain married.

Now, what do you do when your spouse or mate trusts you? The first thing you must do is don't blow it. Once the trust is built and you do something to violate that trust, it will be very hard to get it back. If you have already done something that could destroy the trust in your relationship, you must know that your spouse or partner is going to find out. Whatever is done in the dark will surely come to light. The discovery is even more disturbing when it appears the person whom they trusted hid the information from them. Therefore, you have a decision to make. You can keep silent and hope they never find out or you can confess, suffer the consequences, and work to repair the trust early in the relationship.

You must, however, obtain and retain trust in your marriage and romantic relationships at all cost. That is, if you ever want to really enjoy the lasting beauty of being in a trusting relationship. Even a man who has had sex with many women has never really made love to a woman until he has had sex with a woman who fully trusts him. She will give herself freely without hesitation, reservation and condition. Most women will allow a man to have full access to her body once she has been allowed complete access to his mind. A woman who trusts her man knows that thoughts precede action. She knows he is not going to even think about doing anything that she doesn't like so she will do whatever he asks her to. Now isn't this what every man really wants? Men, isn't this the real reason why we fuss, argue, and don't do what she asks us to do? It's because we feel that she never does what we ask.

The point is if men can do what is required to build or earn a woman's complete trust, she will give her man complete control. The things she has been through with other men in her life (in some cases it will include her father) keeps her from feeling safe enough to trust a man to have control. However, when you love and care for a woman in a way that demonstrates trust consistently, she will yield herself to you completely. To me, that is a good deal. I would give a woman the world if she would just give me two things: trust and peace.

Jesus said in Mark 16:17 "If you only believe", you can perform miraculous things. Believe is the lowest level of relationship that we can have with GOD or man.

So, you see, we do not have to evolve to the highest level of relationship or trust to be empowered to do great things in life for GOD or with our partner. We only need to believe and that belief has the power to change situations and move mountains. However, even with the mountains moving and all of that going on, the relationship will not last forever if it does not reach the level of complete trust.

THE FIVE EMOTIONAL PHASES OF RELATIONSHIPS

The five emotional phases that couples go through as they transition through the various levels of relationships are: ecstasy, reality, challenge, confrontation, and cooperation.

The ecstasy phase is an emotional a state of being, usually at the very beginning of a relationship, where it feels really good to have a new person in our lives. In the ecstasy phase we tend to operate beyond reason or self-control. We don't want to think about anything in this state regardless of how much our friends or relatives try to get us to slow down. We simply want more and more of the ecstasy to the point where we could be swooned or easily be swept off our feet. This state can be dangerous due to the overwhelming emotion or rapturous delight which comes along with it that it could cause us to forsake important things. Some people have decided to give up their children (Susan Smith) to be with a person while in this state which is really a type of trance. Some people even attach a spiritual relevance to it wherein it becomes a kind of a mystic or prophetic trance.

In these instances you will hear a person say that "GOD sent" this person to them. The ecstasy phase is just as addictive as the drug named after it which is a mood-enhancing hallucinogenic amphetamine. A person feels no pain and is really not quite attached to reality while they are in ecstasy.

The reality phase kicks in when something happens to cause the person in ecstasy to suddenly become sober. The hallucinogenic affect of the ecstasy phase wears off and we enter the emotional state of reality. The reality phase is where real people begin to want real answers to real questions. They want to see the reality of the state of affairs they have gotten into and they begin a real live evaluation of the entity they've gotten attached to. In the reality phase a person wants to see if the other person's

Relationships

character or personality is artificial, fraudulent or illusory. They want answers to the concerns that caused reality to kick-in in the first place. They want to know the fundamental and essential things about who this person really is. They want to know if the person is genuinely good and if their relationship really has the potential to be successful.

The challenge phase comes to pass when the person who is seeking real answers cannot get them. The person they are with may simply have issues with allowing others to delve into their private spaces mentally and emotionally or they may just be trying to hide who they really are. Invariably, the person seeking answers becomes frustrated, often times angry, and this leads them to sometimes accuse the other person falsely.

Their problem is they want to know things about which the other person is not being forthcoming. This causes them to order the person to halt, like a guard on sentry duty, in the pursuit of the relationship until they can prove their identity.

Without confrontation there can be no resolution to any problem that we have. The confrontation phase comes after the one seeking answers in the challenge phase becomes angry. If the person doesn't allow themselves to be questioned formally, the other person may resort to confronting or defying them boldly. In most cases, the one who is challenging has become emotionally invested in the other person but they have become uncomfortable with not really knowing who they are. Therefore, they will try to call the person out as a means provoking them to reveal him/her self.

Now, the challenge phase can arise due to other factors such as when one is trying to see what another's intentions are for the relationship. They want to know whether it will lead to marriage, for example, and the other person won't really say or talks as if they are committed but doesn't act like it. However, actions like these drives the person wanting answers to come into a face to face confrontation with the one whom they, in reality, are really trying to love. The challenge and confrontation phases arise as a result of one or both persons resisting mental and/or emotional intimacy.

A couple settles into the cooperation phase once they have obtained intimacy, achieved trust, and are ready to move into marriage. Couples in the cooperation phase begin to act or work together because they want to not because they have to. Their cooperation comes out of a sense of desire to be in harmony and agreement will each other rather than as sense of duty or obligation. They cooperate with each other in a common effort in order to obtain a mutual benefit.

Establish A Prenuptial Agreement

Great cooperation in marriage requires having a good

prenuptial agreement. The process of developing a prenuptial agreement will move a couple quickly from the reality phase into and through the challenge and confrontation phases simultaneously. It will help them to understand very quickly if they have a like vision for their marriage and whether or not they are compatible. If they have difficulty coming to agreement on major issues that are important to them, it will be difficult for them to maintain cooperation in marriage when they actually want or want to achieve different things.

As you can see the prenuptial agreement I am talking about is not the prenuptial hag-greement where a man tries to protect his money just in case his wife becomes a greedy hag. If I were a woman, I would be offended at the suggestion of that type of agreement as well. The prenuptial agreement I believe a couple should draft and sign together is an agreement on how they will live and operate or cooperate as a couple.

This agreement is created before their nuptial proceedings ergo it is a prenuptial agreement. This type of agreement is crucial to the success of a marriage because it helps create a unity of spirit in a bond of peace for the couple prior to their union and prepositions the marriage in mutual agreement. It helps a couple to move into the cooperation phase of a relationship prior to getting married.

Marriage is an institution. Before two people get married, they have to make the decision to become institutionalized. In order to successfully live in an institution, the couple has to have a plan to prevent conflicts and constant confrontations that could drive them crazy. A prenuptial agreement is an operational and organizational plan developed prior to marriage that establishes how a couple will cooperate in marriage. It is crucial for a couple to understand how they intend to operate in marriage before they get married. Trying to devise this plan after they get married tends to keep a couple in the confrontation phase and contributes to the failure of many marriages. Those who fail to plan must plan to fail. People don't plan to fail in marriage they simply fail to plan before marriage.

The purpose of a prenuptial agreement is to lead the couple into unity (u-n–i, with a ty) prior to marriage and help them develop a shared vision for the family. The process of drafting a prenuptial agreement should lead a couple to conclude whether or not there will be unity in their marriage. They should sit down separately and think about every area of marriage imaginable, from love making to housekeeping, and write down how
they view or what they plan to do in that area. They should come together, compare notes, and negotiate any differences in each area until they come into mutual agreement. Next, they should draft a preliminary agreement. Each of them should then spend time alone thinking about whether or not they can live with the terms of the agreement. That is, just in case one of them felt

bullied or intimidated into agreeing to something that they were not really comfortable with. Then, the couple should make their final revisions, draft the final agreement, and both must sign it. The prenuptial agreement is like a business plan for their marriage. It must be kept in an open place where it can be periodically reviewed and followed as their family's guide on how it will cooperate.

THE FIVE CANCERS OF RELATIONSHIPS

The five cancers of a relationship that can surface during the confrontation phase which could kill a couple's ability to build trust and may ultimately cause them to break up are: criticizing, complaining, comparing, competing, and colliding.

Criticizing occurs when one partner begins to consider the merits and demerits of the other partner. Then they begin to judge the person according to their conclusions. Rightly or wrongly they begin to look for and find fault with. Next, they look for any and every opportunity to rebuke for those faults. Hence the reason each time the couple has an argument they bring up the same things every time.

Complaining, also known as nagging, occurs when one partner develops a need to express grief, pain or discontent in the relationship. They are apt to make formal accusations or charges such as lying or cheating.

The complainer is in the midst of an emotional protest or outcry actually because one or more basic needs are not being met. There is ordinarily about 80% truth in the accusations or actions that are being complained about. The one who is being complained about must listen to the complainer rather than try to defend him/her self to discover the need that is not being met. Then they must do whatever they can do to relieve the complainer's grief, pain, or discontent.

Comparing is an act that most women don't like but most men absolutely hate. Comparing is an effort to discover the character or qualities in one's partner by attempting to contrast them with another. That is, usually a former lover. They systematically work to discover resemblances or differences that their partner has with a person they no longer like. Their effort is designed to lead them to conclude that their partner is "just like" Jimmy or "just like" Sue.

In a world where GOD created men and women to be companions they sometimes become competitors. Competing can be good in a relationship where a couple is challenging each other to be the best they can be. Competing becomes corrupting in a relationship when it evolves into a contest as if it were between rivals.
A husband and wife, for example, may compete to see who will gain the upper hand or who will wear the pants in their marriage. There is only one pair of pants allotted

to every marriage. So they strive with one another, both trying to get up earlier than the other, so they can be the one to put on the pants that day.

Colliding comes when the competition is so intense that the couple resorts to injuring each other. Colliding is actually what we call domestic violence. There are times when a woman is truly a victim but there are other times where the woman refuses to be victimized. He hits her out of his frustration over the competition and she hits him back. These people move from being lovers to gladiators. He tries to take the upper hand by using physical force and she responds with direct impact to the gonad sack. If he wants to fight, she is ready to clash.

While violence usually causes one partner to flee I have seen couples who seem to like the violent nature of their relationship. I had a friend tell me that her boyfriend slaps her, she stabs him, and everything is good in their world. She actually told me that if a man doesn't try to beat her every now and then, it means that he is a punk. Then she asked me if she could have sex with me to cheat on her dude whenever she is mad at him. I said, "Noooo". She said, "You punk".

CHEATING: THE ACT THAT BREAKS THE BOND OF TRUST

Cheating or the indiscriminant act of having sex is nothing to people anymore and requires only a very low level of trust. The problem we have in current society in building long lasting relationships based on trust is people jump in bed too quickly. They start bonding physically and chemically before they really get to know each other mentally and spiritually or even establish a moderate level of trust. Since the intent of the act of sex in their heart is not to create a physical, mental and spiritual bond it is easy for a person to leave one and go off to have sex with the next.

When these sexual relationships go wrong it is usually after the woman gets left for another woman. The woman who gets left turns bitter and angry with the man when in reality she was in charge of how the relationship would go. If she simply made the man make a sacrifice to be with her sexually then perhaps it wouldn't have been so easy for him to leave. Women have the power to control the sexual aspects of a relationship. However, what I see too much of is women playing the victim role. Too many of the ladies that I have observed refuse to recognize their role in the failure of that relationship. As Phyllicia Rashad's character said to Kimberly Elise's character in Tyler Perry's movie "For Colored Girls": *"At some point you are going to have to accept some of the responsibility for this. How much you take is up to you, but you will never heal until you accept responsibility for the part you played in it."*

Relationships

Again, a woman's failure to maintain a relationship with the man she has been sleeping with arises in not requiring a man to make any kind of commitment, investment or sacrifice in order to sleep with her. The relationship often goes wrong because she did not lead him to see her value and thus she made it too easy for the guy to leave. GOD built a woman to BE power. Yet, I don't see very many women who recognize that they have this power and very few who actually exercise it.

In the era of free sex the average person sees no duty in taking care and custody of a person's mental, emotional, and in some cases physical, wellbeing. Their habit becomes have sex and then off to the next until they find someone who they really like to have a permanent relationship with. Once they do find someone that they would like to remain with permanently, this is where they begin to have a problem (or so-called sex addiction) because it becomes difficult to break that old habit of jumping from person to person like a rabbit.

Those who decide that they want a permanent relationship try to contain themselves and commit to being with this one person. In the mean time, they don't realize that they have not developed the ability to maintain sexual fidelity. To compound the problem they are becoming chemically bonded in the process of frequently having sex with their decidedly permanent partner. They are setting themselves up to experience a major amount of hurt or

pain. The person whom they decided to love is going to leave because they cannot remain faithful.
Once two people are bonded it hurts whenever they break up or split apart.

There are chemicals or hormones that GOD placed in our bodies that we pass to one another whenever we have sex. These chemicals are designed over time to make two people "literally" become stuck together like glue; a glue in which most women become addicted to. This is why it is very hard for a woman to leave a man that she has been having sex with a long time. The two of them become chemically and spiritually bonded. Once they separate, the chemical and spiritual bond is broken. Like two pieces of paper that have been glued together for a long time, it is hard to take them apart and keep both of them whole or in one piece. If you really want to separate those papers, you end up having to rip them apart. Once people who have been together a long time split up, it is nearly impossible for them to walk away whole. They both become broken or feel ripped apart because there is a tearing of the flesh (chemical composition) and the spirit in the process of separation. This is the scientific reason why it "hurts" when a couple breaks up.

Whitney Houston sang a song "Why Does It Hurt So Bad" that expresses the emotional pain and mental anguish that most people go through once they break up with a person who they've bonded to. At some point they

Relationships

feel like they have mentally moved on but emotionally and spiritually, on a level buried deep inside them, they still feel connected to the person. Therefore, the loss continues to hurt:

"My life's been better

Since the day I left you boy

I must admit life's been kind to me

I went and did the things I said I would boy

I found someone who loves me for me

Haven't had much drama since the day that we split boy

My heart's never been more at ease

And when I think of all the things you put me through

Leaving you has been the best thing for me

Chorus:

So why does it hurt so bad

Why do I feel so sad

I thought I was over you

But I keep crying

When I don't love you

So why does it hurt so bad

Baby I thought I had let you go

So why does it hurt me so

I gotta get you outta my head

Hurts me so bad…"

©Kenny (Baby Face) Edmonds, ECAF Music, Sony ATVSongs, LLC

The chemical and spiritual connection between a couple remains for quite awhile, sometimes years, after they split. The effect of this remaining connection has an emotional effect, more dramatically on a woman, as they meet other people and try to move on. Men were designed to excrete and women were designed to receive so, while men do receive some chemicals from women, women receive much more by comparison. Women, therefore, become chemically bonded (or addicted) to men than men do to women which is one reason why it is easier for men to cheat or just walk away. However, we cannot have sex with a person and just walk away because we will bring the chemicals that we acquired from that person to our other relationships. This is why the conflation of chemicals between a cheating man and woman during sex produces conflagration in his wife. She may not know that her husband is cheating specifically but she can feel it when some other woman is there. There was a chemical transaction that occurred between her husband and another woman. Some of the woman's chemicals get passed to the wife. This is the reason why a woman almost gets sick to her stomach when she finds out that her man is cheating.

The greatest barrier to trust in relationships today is cheating or the fear of cheating. This "fear" causes many women to withhold trust. A man, then, has to know what to do to overcome that fear and lead her to trust. Without that trust a woman can be in a relationship but not be fully present. In those cases she will be reserve in terms of participation and passion because she is trying to keep herself from being hurt.

The way to overcome fear and obtain trust is through love. "There is no fear in love; but perfect love casts out fear… (1 John 4:18)." Most women need this type of love in order to give a man their trust. She needs to know that he is not going to leave, stray or betray her trust.

A man will never really know the true pleasure of making love until he makes love to a woman who really trusts him enough to open up and fully release her heart and soul to him. When a man cheats or makes his woman feel that he is cheating he makes her close herself off to him. They may still remain together but she does not remain open. Cheating is not actually seeking the pleasure of love but rather the love of pleasure. Men who seek the love of pleasure have never known the pleasure of love. A man will never fully know the pleasure of love until he overcomes the love of pleasure. What he has been chasing in the street, the pleasure of love, has been at home all the time. However, he can never find it at home until he becomes faithful and loving enough to lead his wife to completely trust him. If he gives her what she needs, she will give him all the pleasure that he wants.

Chapter 2
THE ESSENTIAL ELEMENTS OF LOVE

"Love doesn't claim possession, but gives freedom."
~ **Rabindranath Tagore**

There are many elements of love. However, there are only three essential elements of love: freedom, justice and equality.

To be essential means a thing would cease to be what it is without that element or elements. An essential element of cake is sugar. A cake without sugar is only bread. Without the essential element, despite one's best efforts to mix and knead them together, the other elements alone would not become cake. Similarly, without the essential elements of freedom, justice and equality love would not become love despite one's best efforts to build it. It will only become abuse.

Ecclesiastes 4:12 helps us to see that real love is like a three-fold cord that is not easily broken. One cord alone is much easier to break than three cords woven together. It is much harder for a couple to break up that is intertwined in love after they have given each other the 3-fold cord of freedom, justice and equality. On the other hand, relationships that lack the essential elements or that are not bound by the three cords of love break apart when under intense pressure.

Freedom is present in love when each person is free to be who GOD created them to be. A woman is free in love when she does not have to hide her strengths to protect her husband's weaknesses. A man is free in love when he can work as long as he feels he needs to provide for his family and advance his career without his wife constantly complaining about him not being home enough.

Justice is present in love when the rules that apply to one in the relationship apply to both. If a man wants to stay out with his friends all night, there should be no problem if his wife does the same thing. That would be just. If a woman wants to pick or comment on the clothes her husband wears or demand that he not hang out with certain friends, her husband should not be accused of being controlling if he picks her clothes or friends.

Equality is present in love when one is not elevated over or made more important than the other. A wife's career, hopes and aspirations, for example, should not be put on hold until after her husband accomplishes his. A woman who wants her husband to have hard pecks and washboard abs should be tight in those areas also. The standard that one has for their mate should be the same standard that they maintain themselves.

When the essential elements of freedom, justice and equality are present in a relationship then love can grow and become what it was truly meant to be. What is birthed out of true love, then, is a combination of caring, commitment, responsibility, and respect. These elements provide the platform on which to build trust. Without trust a marriage is always one disagreement or indiscretion away from divorce. Without love and trust in a relationship or marriage it will eventually lead to cheating.

WHY DO MEN CHEAT?

A theory that explains one of the reasons why men cheat is called "The Dirt Theory".

The Dirt Theory centers on the fact that GOD created men from the dirt. Thus men have a tendency to gravitate toward the dirt. This is why men are bottom line oriented in problem solving, want to get to the heart of a matter, or uncover the root cause. This is also why, ladies, when you are explaining something to a man, he is not interested in the details. A man has an innate desire to get to the "bottom" (pardon the pun) of things quickly or back to the dirt.

Watch the behavior of a little boy who has just been given a bath and dressed in clean clothes. His first instinct is to go outside and play in the dirt. The desire to get to the dirt is the reason some men will try to have sex with a woman as quickly as he can after meeting her. He wants to get to the bottom line, if you will, to see if she will do all the "dirty" little things that his wife or woman will not. The desire to get to the dirt is the reason why a man could leave home and lie down with some dirty woman who couldn't hold a candle to his wife. SOME men tend to love to lie with dirty women as adults as much as we loved to play in the mud as boys. Rooting around in dirt is just part of a man's nature.

This is not an excuse for a man to use or for a woman to excuse cheating. It is just one theory.

A second theory that explains why men cheat is called "The Because They Can Theory".

The reason some men act like (what some women call) "dogs" and have sex with several other women is because they can. The reason they do and can is because the women they are with tolerate it and the women whom they cheat with allow it. How many women do you know that are dealing with a man who they know already has another woman? How many women do you know that make a regular habit of having sex with a man within a short time of meeting him? Sometimes they don't know much about the guy or even his "real" name before they have sex with him. Many women who catch their man cheating will often remain with him thus giving tacit approval to the behavior. Some women have even caught their man with other women several times yet still chose to remain with him. This activity breeds dog like behavior in men. Men who cheat frequently are likely those who suffer no real consequences for their actions. They cheat, therefore, because they can.

Ironically, most women know instinctively when the man they are with is sneaking around but they allow him to continue while they wait for confirmation. Once a woman who is merely dating a man gets confirmation that should be enough to stop allowing a cheating man to waste minutes of her life with him that once lost she can never get back. Allowing him to remain with you will be condoning his cheating ways, expose you to anything nasty that she might have, and position him to block you from finding someone who will really be good to and do right by you.

There is no up-side for a woman who seeks to salvage a relationship with a man who is "tippin'" out with tricks. I understand that if a woman is married to a cheating man, it becomes much more complicated. Just walking away may not be an option particularly when children are involved. In either case, walking away will not be easy. However, when a man is dating a woman and decides to have sex with another woman it means that he "really" wants to be with her. Ergo, it is best to allow him to have his desire and leave him alone.

Relationships

A third theory that attempts to explain why some men cheat is called "The Reproductive Mutation Theory".

Men typically have an X and Y chromosome in each of the cells of their bodies that determine sex. Women typically have two X chromosomes. Metaphorically, the X and Y chromosomes represent the spiritual and physical nature of human beings with the upper half being the spiritual and the lover half being the physical. The upper half is symbolic of an individual with their arms reaching toward the heavens. The lower half is symbolic of how an individual positions their feet as they stand on the earth. The X represents an individual with feet in a wide stance and the Y represents an individual standing that is missing one leg. The X represents a structure with a firm foundation that is able to stand when rocked. The Y represents an unbalanced structure that is easily toppled over when rocked and therefore needs support; it needs help at times to stand.

In male and female twin sets, the female more often than not will begin to walk first. The female has always been the more stable of the sexes. The woman has always been more concerned about home, family, and security. Women have always wanted to provide their children with a foundational structure in which to grow that is sure or firm and secure. Women have always looked to their husbands to help provide that firm foundation. The problem is men are internally wobbly and need help to stand.

Each fetus begins from a female egg fertilized by a male sperm. Thus each fetus begins as female or with XX chromosomes. After about 6 weeks of development a gene called SRY impacts one of the X chromosomes, cuts off one of its long stems (or legs), and changes it to a Y. This causes the sex organs to fall. The inner ovaries become external testes. The short stem clitoris becomes a long stem penis. The transmutation or fall internally to produce the male sexual identity makes a man inherently unstable and subject to fall. He develops a strong desire to procreate as a consequence of this process through a psychosomatic (psycho-chromo-somatic) need to feel strong and whole again. He instinctively understands that his source of power, getting back that whole X, is through women. There was a sex related process that caused his organs to fall so he intuitively knows that there is a sex related process involved in becoming whole or being able to stand on the inside.

Women are higher beings technologically than men. As a result of being stronger internally, women can do many things better than men. Women have better motor, verbal, cognitive, and organizational skills than men. Women can do most everything that a man can do but men can't do everything a woman can. The only disadvantage that women have comparatively is their lack of great upper body strength. Thus women need the man's external power and men need the woman's internal power. Men have an inherent desire to access this power. When this desire becomes excessive it turns into a type of lust which leads to cheating. Cheating for some men is a psychosomatic need to feel whole or powerful though having sex with many women.

A fourth theory that attempts to explain why some men cheat is called "The Because He Resents You Theory."

Resentment often develops towards a person who is helping in the person being helped as a result of pride, low self esteem, or a sense of lacking. At some point, the person being helped concludes the person helping them thinks they are better than them. Male resentment towards women begins with boys and their mothers and it transfers to their girlfriends and wives. Mothers today take care of boys too much, love them too much, try to protect them too much, serve them too much, and give them too much. Mothers who do this think that it will make their boys love, respect, and appreciate them more.

The opposite result manifests because boys that have everything done for them grow up to be a weak dependent and never learn how to be a strong man. I have a nephew who was on parole at the time he was being kicked out of his girlfriend's house. As I was trying to explain to him what it takes for a man to live with a woman in terms of knowledge and ability, he realized that he didn't know and couldn't do a thing. He tearfully said to me "I think my mother ruined me". I felt for him. Although he needed to take some responsibility for his condition what he said was true. This boy never had to do a thing at home. He was well into his teen years before his mother stopped washing his back when he took a bath. She only stopped then because I led her to see that she was making her boy a dependent and that no other woman was going to do all of the things that she was doing for him.

Some men grow to resent women simply because they try to help them too much. A woman will allow an adult male to live in her home who had no income, no job, and no assets when she took him in. She takes care of him like he is a boy so he doesn't actually feel like a man. Predictably, he goes out with "the boys" to find other women to be with who certify his manhood. He actually resents the woman who is taking care of him because she treats him like a boy in many cases such as dictating when and under what conditions he can use the car. She knows this big boy is not a man so sets rules for him in the house and a time when he should be home at night. Does a woman who has a man like this really expect him to be a man when he is being treated like a boy? For some reason women do expect him to be a man even though they know that he is only a man-sized boy. They get angry and start saying things like "Be a man!" which is like yelling at a car "Be a truck!" If that big boy knew how to be a man, he wouldn't have to have someone to force him to be. He would just be.

In reality, guys like this don't have to be a man because there will always be a woman somewhere who will take care of him. There will always be a woman somewhere who will be turned on by his "boyish" charms. Once the woman who is taking care of him currently begins to make too many demands that the boy be a man, he will lash out and she will put him out. But now he has another woman who thinks his helplessness is cute. She will take him in and the cycle begins again. He will start to resent her, begin to hang out with other women who make him feel like a man, he will lash out and get put out.

The final theory that I'll present which explains why men cheat is the "Sexual Addiction Theory".

The things that men find sexy and/or attractive about some women are the reason why they want them or will cheat on their wives with but it is also the reason why they leave them. When a relationship starts out with sex it is going to end because the person who wanted sex with them will want sex with someone else.

The act of sex is simply the manifestation of the lust that is living in a person's heart. The lust that one had for the one they are with is going to be directed toward another when the lust wanes for the one they are with. Lust always wants more and more. It is never satisfied. Lust is always looking for something different and more and more of something different. Men who are married that frequently cheat are said to be dealing with an addiction sex. However, the reality is they have an addiction to lust. It is not so much the sex that they want as it is the lust that is driving them desire more and more sex with different people.

A relationship cannot begin in sex or in lust if it is to last out of bed. Once women who are looking for love stop just giving into the lust that is in a man's heart, it will cause men to make better choices. Men will be forced to be more selective of the women they deal with because it will cost them a commitment. Men place no value on women who give themselves away cheaply. It is nice to get sex or free booty. However, men won't stick around for very long if they see the woman beginning to act like she wants a commitment.

If a woman will do a lot of things for or with a man that the woman he loves won't do, he will keep having sex with her as long as she allows him to. However, he will never leave the one he loves for her no matter how many promises he might make. The woman he is satisfying his lust with will pressure him to leave his love to keep his lust. She does this just so that she can feel that she is not being used. But at the end of the day, he is not going to leave his love and she will have no choice but to recognize that she was being used. Then she will want to take revenge somehow and cause him to lose his love. She will want to hurt the man's love simply because she was only the object of lust.

Ladies must understand that the woman who is the object of a man's lust always gets left. Google any study yourself and you will find that a lustful man rarely marries his mistress. In the cases where they do wed, 75% of those marriages end in divorce. The woman who is the subject of a man's love on the other hand never or rarely gets left.

Therefore, a woman who really wants love cannot allow a relationship to begin in lust. She cannot walk around half naked and expect a man who meets her to begin thinking about love and commitment when she is displaying that she is available to be an avenue through which he can satisfy his lust.

In reality, only man-sized boys are attracted to the half naked not real men. If you want a real man who will begin thinking about making a commitment upon meeting you, you must cover up your curves and give him a little mystery. That will make him want to see what is in your heart and mind. His objective will be to discover what it will take to get you to accept his plans for taking your hand in marriage so that he can unwrap that package.

WHY DO WOMEN CHEAT?

The theory that explains why women cheat is "The Spiritual Response Theory". The Spiritual Response Theory states the reason why women cheat is in response to men cheating. A man gives a woman only three options when he cheats on her: to stay, to leave, or to cheat too.

Whatever a man has in his heart and his spirit was designed by GOD to transfer to his wife. That was done so that the two of them can become one of heart or mind and spirit. The act or process of intercourse causes the two to become one so whatever is in him will be passed into her. The woman was designed to reproduce after the man's kind. Therefore, whatever is in him is going to be reproduced through her.

When a man retains lust in his heart and spirit from his promiscuous ways before marriage it produces a desire for excess in the marriage. For some this could lead to excessive drinking, or gambling, but for others to cheating. Overtime, the activity of intercourse will cause the lust in a man's heart or spirit to pass from him to his wife. This places the spirit of lust or excess desire into her. Thus, some women develop the excess desire to have other men too. However, this lust and excess desire can manifest itself in other ways. This is why some women who choose to stay with their cheating husbands often resort to excessive drinking, gambling, shopping, prescription drug use, etc.

Now, couple the Spiritual Response Theory with the acceptance in modern society of women having several sexual partners before they were married who were

Relationships

mainly attracted to them through the spirit of lust and you can see how it plants the spirit of cheating or lust and excess in the women of a society generally. This activity over time overrides the "program", if you will, that women were designed with by GOD to be faithful and to desire only her husband.

"…and thy desire shall be to thy husband… (Genesis 3:16)."

Therefore, the old African proverb becomes true "If you go into an area where you can't find any good women, it is filled with no good men." The order of any activity, community or organization (such as marriage and sexual activity) always begins with men. It appears that we are caught in a perpetual paradox wherein the women need to stop giving it up so that the men can step up. Many of us seem to think that if the women don't set a standard, men have no incentive to rise up to standards. However, the reverse is actually true. Men are supposed to establish the order in a home or community and women are supposed to maintain it. When the order is established properly by men the women happily maintain it and teach their children to adhere to it. Whether they like to admit it or not every strong woman wants a strong man. When a man stands strong a strong woman will stand with and even behind him.

Whenever women and children are out of order it is

because the men are not doing what they should do or are not standing in their proper place. Men can stop the cheating and abuse in their communities by not having sex with any woman who is not his wife. Whenever a woman to whom he is not married tries to seduce him, he must keep his power under control and tell her no! Just because a woman wants to give it, it does not mean that a man has to take it. I've conditioned my mind to see every woman as some proud papa's baby girl. So I wouldn't do anything to any man's daughter that I wouldn't want another man to do to my baby girl. Men must understand that having sex outside of wedlock is engaging in the abnormal use or abuse of a woman. If a man doesn't cheat, there is a very good probability that his wife won't cheat either. The average woman really only wants to be with that one man whom she can love and trust.

WOMEN HAVE THE POWER TO PUT AN END TO CHEATING MEN

Finding out that a spouse or lover has cheated is a significant life event for many people which causes some to experience a type of grief. The shock of the event leads a person to rationalize it and to find a cause or place to assign blame. I've often heard the friends of a person going through this asking their friend why they are focusing the blame on the other person involved rather than their lover. The reason they blame the other person is first due to denial that their spouse or lover would do that to them. Second they are having difficulty facing the reality that they were betrayed therefore the lover or spouse is not the one who they initially blame. When the shock that precedes grief strikes we tend to react like a person who just got shot. They felt the impact, they can see the blood, but shock causes the mind to deny that it happened. Once grief kicks in the mind allows them to process the reality of what happened and they will say something like "You shot me!"

The Kübler-Ross model of the progression or stages of grief are:

1. Denial - This can't be happening, not to me.
2. Anger - How can this happen to me; Who is to blame?
3. Bargaining – I know I need to leave but I have to stay until the children graduate.
4. Depression – What's the point; why go on?
5. Acceptance – I have to prepare to leave now; we can work through it.

The problem with grief is it is just as much of a killer as cancer. Grief can in fact lead to death via suicide and cardiac arrest or what some call a broken heart if

depression becomes acute. Grief is also a killer in terms

of creativity and productivity therefore it could kill a person's career professionally. Grief can kill a person's will and self-esteem as well as alter their personality. It will make a person who was once perfectly fit fat and one who was wealthy poor. Since cheating can cause grief and have such a powerful impact on a woman's well being, there should be an annual parade, walk or crusade (as with breast cancer) to fight against cheating.

Women in America represent 53% of the population and just over 50% of the working population. That means women have over half of the money in this country. Some women that have an ex-husband some with a "baby daddy" have even more money because they have all of theirs and half of his. Large amounts of money and large groups of people are the two main forms of power. Therefore, women have the means to finance any mission or cause that they want. Without a single vote from a man women could elect the next President all on their own if they decided to get together and utilize their power. For some reason women don't seem to recognize how to organize and utilize their power to advance their position in the country.

I may get some feminists types to complain that I'm beating up on women or blaming the victim. But because I know that women are actually very powerful I have to say this. I believe it is time for women to step into their

Relationships

power, stop playing the victim, and begin to just be powerful. What I am saying is no different than what your brother would say who is tired of seeing you messing around with men who constantly cheat on you.

The feminists are really the problem because they are the ones who have been keeping women from ending the relationship madness that they experience with men at home and in the work place by positioning women as poor little victims. It has already been proven, time and time again, that there are some things that women do better than men. It has already been proven that women can do things like construction work that men previously thought they couldn't do. Women have the power and ability to do whatever they want to do and to be whatever they want to be. People who act like victims tend to be victimized. Perhaps this is the reason why women still only earn 77% of what men earn even when doing the same job. Women must begin to seize power, recognize their value at work and at home, and stop allowing the feminists to frame them as victims.

The question is, then, since women actually have the power but appear unwilling to use it at what point do we begin to hold them responsible for the choices they make? The feminist position is that a woman should never be held responsible for what men do to them. However, absent physical violence a man cannot do anything to a woman that she does not allow him to do. I marvel at how beautifully powerful women are. Yet, many women don't seem to recognize their power and utilize it. A woman is a very powerful vehicle who can take a man anywhere he wants to go as long as he knows how to handle her. That includes her boss as well as her husband. Every Fortune 500 corporation grew to be an economic giant because there was a woman in there somewhere nurturing it and causing it to grow. Therefore, a woman has to teach a man how to recognize her value both in the work place and at home so that she won't be mistreated. A woman who teaches the men around her how she wants to be treated will never be mistreated and will rarely be cheated on.

When it comes to dating, love, and marriage a woman has to set a standard, demand a commitment, and never allow a man to have sex her who is not her husband. If she never demonstrates that she loves herself, he will not be able to find a reason to love her. If she says she is Christian but allows a man who is not her husband to have her, he will conclude in his mind that if he can take her away from Jesus, any other man will be able to take her away from him. A woman must demonstrate that she has value in order for a man to value her. If he sees no value in her, it will be easy for him leave her.

I have a friend. She and the father of her two children were living together. They broke up because she asked him why he loves her and he couldn't tell her. It upset her that he could find no value in their relationship other than it was convenient for him. Too many of my female friends are so gorgeous, talented, and intelligent but when it comes to building and maintaining relationships most of them just don't get it. They give men all the benefits of marriage without requiring them to make a marriage commitment. These women do everything for these men that a wife would do, including having babies, but they have no husband. They often get left or force the man to leave because they make it too easy for him to walk away. I believe relationships between women and men are not going to change until women begin to utilize their power. They need to step out of the feminist echo chamber with their girlfriends and start listening to men who love them like their dads, brothers, uncles, cousins, etc. Cheating is not going to stop until women begin to utilize their power. Men have a GOD ordained responsibility to control the sexual activity in their communities but women make it too easy for men to shirk their responsibility by giving sex away too freely.

The main reason why men cheat as I said before is because they can! There is always a woman around somewhere who will cheat with them. There is always a woman around somewhere who will live with them, believe the lies, give him another chance, or hold out hope that he will change. In the end men like these (who are not really men at all, merely boys who are man-sized) don't have to change because the women in their lives do not establish a high standard of conduct and adhere to it.

Women today seem to be so afraid of being alone that they will put up with anything. They don't really understand why the men in their lives cheat particularly when they are trying to be the best woman they can for him. Women get together occasionally to complain about cheating men but men will never stop cheating unless women stop forgiving them and taking them back in.

That said women are receiving a barrage of criticism of late in the social media because it is really long overdue. Thanks to the feminine activists there has been a lot of man bashing since the late 80's proclaiming all men are dogs, talk of dead beat dads, and so on, which most men didn't argue with because we knew it was true. True, that is, not for all men but for many. Now, as the tables turn and the men begin to criticize women for their participation in the men's dog like behavior they cry foul, refuse to listen, and storm off. For whatever reason women seem to believe that they are above reproach. Women seem to feel that they do not have to take responsibility for relationships going sour and do not have to share any of the blame when a pregnancy occurs. It's the man's fault so he must pay the price. The relationship then goes bad and the child they had suffers.

Now, there is one thing that all women can agree on. When it comes to sex men are stupid. Not some, all. Men

Relationships

have to be trained, taught and guided into pleasing a woman the way in which "she" wants to be pleased otherwise she will only get treated like the last chick he was with.If you don't tell him what you like, he will be doing what she liked. But in the lead up to the sexual act men can go from Mr. Nice to Mr. Nasty in the time it takes to snap a finger. The command control center moves from the big head to the little head within the space of a heart beat. The one-eyed trouser trout is now at the helm guiding the USS Beef Cake to dock into a warm water port. At this point the man knows what he is doing and can see himself doing it but he is really not in control. In situations where the man doesn't usually get any, he is actually having an out of body experience. It is like he is there watching somebody else having this experience with his body. Once his inner essence is released, however, all of his mental faculties come flooding very quickly back to reality.

The reality here is this boy was stupid. Anyone of average intelligence knows that having sex could potentially produce a baby. The problem with this guy is he was trying to get to have sex with the lady but wasn't planning to make a baby. The second problem is he had unprotected sex with her. Four months later she tells him that they are expecting a baby. Mr. stupidity freaks out then says and does some things that he really didn't mean. The shock of the announcement "I'm pregnant" strikes a man who wasn't planning to have a baby like a bullet to the gut. The reality of that news causes a type of grief in men once they realize that they must carry the responsibility of being a father. He doesn't want to be a father but the lady wants to be a mommy and she is determined to have this baby.

The sudden realization that he is going to be a father causes the grief process to begin in a man who really is not ready to be a daddy. This is why the man first goes into denial: you can't be pregnant; it can't be mine. Then anger: how could this be happening to me; how could you do this to me; you set me up. Next, bargaining: are you going to have the baby; do you want me to pay for the abortion? Once he realizes that she is going to have the baby and there is nothing he can do about it he goes into depression. Now, some men never emerge from the depressed stage of grief so they never want to have anything to do with the lady or the baby. Most men who do emerge from the depression stage move into acceptance. They try to make the best of the situation for the sake of the child. The problem now is the damage they did to the woman emotionally as they were going through the denial, anger, and depression stages of grief.

Sometimes women are hurt badly when they see a man react wildly to the news of pregnancy. They expect a man, who wasn't planning to have a baby to be happy about it immediately, become a family man instantly, and just take on all of the responsibility for the child financially.

Relationships

We did agree earlier that most men are stupid right? Everybody knows that having sex can ultimately lead to having a baby. However, men who say that they are "fooling around" with a young lady are really only doing just that. They are just fooling around. There is nothing serious about their relationship with her other than getting some serious… whatever. Most men who are not married to a woman but are sleeping with them don't plan to have children with them. What he doesn't understand is that she is having sex with him hoping that sex will lead to long lasting love. So when she becomes pregnant, she wants to own the choice for taking that pregnancy to term but she really wants him to want to bear the responsibility for her and the baby. Why, because that is what she expected him to do before she decided to start sleeping with him. The problem is (in a low whisper) that is not what was on his mind at all. She was looking for love but all he wanted was sex. Helen Rowland, author of "Reflections of a Bachelor Girl", said: "To a woman the first kiss is just the end of the beginning but to a man it is the beginning of the end."

Yes, there are some boys who try to get girls pregnant but there are women who also get pregnant intentionally because they want a baby or they want to keep a man. When men who don't want to be a father go through their angry phase they conclude that the woman got pregnant on purpose. Women become furious at that suggestion because they were thinking "He wants to have sex with me because he loves me." Nooo, he just loved having sex with her. Grief starts to beset her now and she gets angry once she realizes that it was just a sex game for him. She begins to regret all the times that she was trying to make the sex fun and intriguing by calling him to come over and have sex or showing up late nights at his place for a booty call. You see, some women in this situation will recognize that they led the man to believe that the sex was all fun and games too. Still, once she gets pregnant she has no choice but to try to make the man get serious, if not about her, at least for the baby.

The problem is he was never serious about her and he never wanted a baby in the first place. Therefore, he is not going to get serious about her after a pregnancy pops up that he didn't want. The only thing she gets from him initially is anger and resentment. Once she realizes that she can't bargain with this guy for acceptance of her and the baby, grief causes her to go into the depression stage. Therefore, the man in her mind becomes a dog, she separates from him, takes off with the baby, and he becomes a dead beat. Some women never emerge from the depression stage which is fueled by a cycle of anger and sporadic fits of rage.

I put that scenario together to illustrate that women have to start taking responsibility for the choices they make beginning with whom they choose to have sex. At some point women must start listening to men about

Relationships

how to deal with men rather than just their girlfriends! Too many of your girlfriends think that luring a man into a sexual relationship gives them the authority to make him see them exclusively. However, a man will tell you that you can't give yourself away for free but then expect a man to see you as valuable. A man is not going to sacrifice his freedom and invest the rest of his life in a woman who appears to place no value on herself. He will have sex with her but he won't marry her. He will keep having sex with her until someone who he believes has real value comes along. I understand that this is a paradox but women must change in order for men to change! Men are supposed to lead but they have abdicated their responsibility to lead in order to obtain free sex. Therefore, women must stop given themselves away for free. Then men will more than likely return to their responsibility.

The place where this child out of wedlock relationship dynamic can be seen more prominently than any other is within the black community. According to the US Census, 43% of black women have never been married and over 70% of black children are born to single mothers. Orlando Patterson, Sociology Professor Harvard University, states that 60% of African American children live without the emotional, disciplinary, or economic help of their father. He also found that black couples have the lowest rate of marriage than any other racial group, the highest rate of divorce, the highest rate of co-habitation, and the highest rate of co-habitation break-ups. Even black couples are just living together they can't seem to stay together. So why is it that blacks are not marrying at the rate of other groups and when they do marry, they break up?

A study conducted by Linda J. Waite and Kara Joyner of the Population Research Center, Univ. of Chicago, "Men and Women's General Happiness and Sexual Satisfaction in Marriage, Cohabitation and Single Living" shows that there are other issues that contribute to this malady within the black community such as low or no employment among black men that makes them feel they are not ready or diminishes their eligibility in the eyes of black women. However, one of the main reasons why black couples have so much difficulty getting and remaining married is because black women, for the most part, are still following the women's liberation movement. Wealthy white women abandoned that ship a long time ago. They know that it leads to divorce. The liberation movement places children at risk for poverty, drug use, crime, suicide and incarceration. That is why these issues are affecting black communities across the nation compared to others disproportionately. Women's liberation destroys families and hurts children because the liberation theology defies the order of GOD for the family.

According to the Centers for Disease Prevention and Control and the National Institute of Health 16% of all children were born out of wedlock in America between 1950 and 1954. At the start of the Women's Liberation

Movement, between 1970 and 1974, that number increased to 34%. Subsequently, out of wedlock births have remained level nationally since 1979 at 40%. That rate has been holding steady because a lot of women have recognized that the liberation theology is injurious to women and families. But given the fact that black women didn't seem to get the memo and continue to follow the liberation theology all national social and economic maladies affect blacks disproportionately. Black out of wedlock birth rate today is at 72% and increasing annually. The same percent of black children in America live in poverty. These statistics are a direct result of adherence to the liberation movement.

There is also a great deal of confusion within male and female relationships in America because most of US don't know that there are two women's movements operating simultaneously with conflicting ideals. One was designed to free women from inequality and the other was designed to free women from their traditional gender roles. Those movements are: The Women's Movement and the Women's Liberation Movement. The Women's Movement was designed to achieve equality; equal pay for equal work and so on. Its mantra is "We want to be treated equally with men". The Women's Liberation movement was designed to prove that a woman can do anything that a man can do and that being treated "like" a woman was socially and professionally degrading. Its mantra is "We want to be treated like men".

Having these two movements operating simultaneously drives men crazy because they have a hard time figuring out what to do. Some things they do women like but if they do the same thing with another woman she gets offended. The reason some women want doors opened for them and some don't depends upon which movement they follow. You will hear women who follow the liberation movement say "We are just like men". However, that is the crux of the problem. A woman can do the job that a man does but she should never allow herself to be "just like" a man. First, it is not attractive and second two dudes make dodo! When there are two dudes in the home there is always going to be some $hit. They will always vie against one another for domination, leadership, or to be the head.

Anything with two heads is a monster. Monster type relationships either die early naturally as they are defective genetically or they must be killed because they are dangerous to children. As a result of some women strongly following the liberation movement, they are doing every damnable thing that a man would do and are going to hell in a hand basket just like the men are. The problem is the children are going too!

The US Department of Justice Bureau of Prison Statistics reports the fastest growing prison demographic in America is among women who have children under 18. Many of these children have fathers who are in jail as well. So what do you think is going to happen to the great majority of these children? Hooray for you ladies! You've come a long way baby. You are now "just like men"! You can now do everything that men do including drinking, sexing, drugging, hanging in bars late at night, working late everyday and not spending enough time with your children. But the kids are paying the price for it and your relationships with their fathers are either suffering or nonexistent because of it. When men see or feel like they have to deal with another man at home they are going to go out and look for a woman. The liberation theology breaks up families and it also creates the environment that makes women available with free sex for husbands to run to.

Again, one of the main reasons why men cheat is because they can. Liberation has made it easy for him. If a man's wife won't do what he wants there is always a woman around somewhere who knows he has another woman that will cheat with him. There is always a woman around somewhere who will live with a cheating man, believe his lies, give him another chance, and hold out hope that he will change. In the end men like these don't have to change because the women in their lives do not demand a high standard of conduct. So the question is what are you going to do? Women have the power to stop cheating men in their tracks simply by discarding the liberation theology and demanding a standard of conduct that they won't deviate from.

Also, a lot of women today don't really seem to care if a man is unfaithful. They don't really want a real relationship with the man whom they are having sex with. They only want an opportunity to get their freak on regularly. The National Vital Statistics Report "Births: Final Data for 2007" issued by the Centers for Disease Control revealed that older women were beginning to outpace teens in having babies. This means that the older liberation era women are still out there getting their freak on without demanding a standard of marriage before a man can have sex with them.

Real women already know that in order to attract a real man she must sacrifice sex. A woman's value is connected to her virtue. In a real man's mind a woman who just gives herself away has no value. Men neither value nor respect women who give themselves away for free. They will have sex with her while they continue to play the field looking for something "better" to come along who they can have enough respect for to marry. Men who begin to play the "something better" game cheat because they discover the woman was not the person that she appeared to be. So, they go back out in the field looking for something better. Another reason why they cheat is because they have not learned and do not have any incentive to be faithful. Remember ladies, if you run into a real man and you would like to have him just for you, don't give him none! Then he will want to talk to you to try to discover your value. If he likes it then he's gonna put a ring on it.

Relationships

Ladies, men don't become faithful they must be made faithful. Infidelity is a character flaw that is either led, trained or beat out of a young boy by his dad. Men who have not learned to be faithful though close association with other men will have a difficult time becoming faithful on their own. This is especially true in today's socio-sexual environment thanks to the liberation movement. Men have no incentive to even try to be faithful because there is no real price that they have to pay for infidelity. Once a man is caught most women forgive him and continue on having sex with him. Women can guide a man into being faithful by establishing a standard and making him pay if he plays. A woman who wants a faithful man must also set a standard for the men that he associates with. If he is married, she must ensure that he terminates close associations with single men and create stronger ties with family men. Other happily married men will help keep his eyes focused on home, loving you, and helping raise the kids.

Chapter 3
LOVE BUILDING BASICS

"Love doesn't make the world go 'round. Love is what makes the ride worthwhile." ~ Franklin P. Jones

There are some things we absolutely must know in order to build and maintain a lasting love relationship. For instance, as we will discuss in the Men Versus Women chapter, men and women have attributes that are inherent to each gender. If you do not know and understand what these attributes are, why they are gender specific, and why we have them they can drive you crazy.

Women that are mothers are called "Ma". The word Ma is a Hebrew word that means "to push". The word Ma is appropriate for a woman because it is in her nature to push. She tries to push her husband to greatness on his job and in his personal endeavors. We men call it nagging but she is pushing. She tries to push the children to do well in school and in their extracurricular activities. When a woman asks her husband to do a chore or a job for her, she pushes him to do it right away. Why; because it is in a woman's nature to push. If a man does not understand that it is in a woman's nature to push, the pushing she does to get him to do what she needs is going to drive him crazy.

Relationships

Men that are fathers are called "Dad". The word DAD is an acronym that means a delayed action device. It is inherent in a man's nature to pause and contemplate before he does anything. GOD put this delay switch in men because Adam reacted impulsively to Eve's pushing. Whenever a woman is pushing a man to do whatever it is that she wants him to do, he is going to do it, only he will delay first. If a woman does not understand that this delay is inherent in the nature of a man, it could drive her crazy or make her think that he does not care how she feels.

Therefore, when a person seeks to be married or wants to create a long lasting relationship with someone they must understand the nature of that person's gender. They must obtain a great deal of understanding on what both men and women do in relationships and why so that they don't go into it without knowledge and end up hurt and confused. They must conduct a thorough self assessment and get to know their own strengths and weaknesses as well as their gifts, talents and abilities. They must also have a strong grasp on what they want to do in life; their goals and aspirations. Then they must know how their strengths and weaknesses will complement another person. Knowing who you are, what you want to do, and what you have to offer will reveal to you the type of person who you will be able to complement. The type of person who you can complement is the only type that will be right for you. Next, make an assessment of the qualities and characteristics of the type of person who you will be right for will possess. Then, set out to find that type of person. You will see people who you want but they won't be right. You will meet people who want you but do not settle for anyone just because they are available. That person will be occupying the position of the person you really need, the right one, or the one who will truly complement you.

Dating, the way in which it is normally done today, is not an option for the person who wants to find and marry Mr. or Ms. Right. One of the reason it is hard for some to get married is because they don't know how to date. Dating is not a process of occupying one's space and time for entertainment purposes. True dating is a process of moving toward a wedding date. Whenever you go on a date today, whether you are male or female, you must realize that at the end of that date (the way that dating is done today) you are going to get left. Your date may last for one night, one week, one month, or 15 years, but at the end of a date your lover will leave you. Again, the true purpose of dating is to plan a move or set a course to reach a wedding date. Spending time and energy with a person who is not interested in an engagement and formulating a plan to complete that engagement on a date certain will be a waste of time. You could have used that time to develop a plan to marry someone who is serious about marrying you. Participating in dating as it is done today is in effect consenting to allow another person to use you for their entertainment or pleasure until they are ready to move on.

Relationships

The people you are dating that have not made a commitment and set a wedding date are in reality planning to leave you. Regardless of what they say with their mouths, their actions say otherwise. So, never let someone occupy your time while they are trying to find the one who they really want. Both men and women like to play this game, but men are masters. Women are more apt to keep a man she has been dating for a long time. She knows he is not really right for her but she will try to make him into the type of man that she really wants. However, men will hold on to a woman that he can have sex with. That is, until a new woman or the type of woman that he really wants comes along.

Ladies, men who play the dating game (which is really a sex game) always put women whom they date in one of three categories. A man knows within a short period of time what file he is going to place a woman in: family, friend, or freak. If you've been dating a man beyond 2-3 months and he is not already talking about marriage, you are not in the family file. If you are having sex with him, you are not in the friend file. This means you are in the freak file. Therefore, you will be used for sex until he finds a woman who he wants to put in the family file. Life is too short to be dating, going together, or fooling around if your goal is to actually be married. The only time you should be "going with" someone is when you are going to the altar. So, don't waste too much time with someone who is really not ready to be married or who is not really interested in marrying you. This is why it is not good to have sex before marriage. When we leave someone with whom we had been having sex it can cause mental, physical, and emotional damage in their heart. We often leave a long trail of people who we have done wrong when we are just having sex with someone until the right one comes along. Too often we cannot find the right one because we are not finished paying for the one's we've done wrong.

I understand the way that I am explaining the dating process is totally counter to modern day sensibilities but this is why our relationships, especially marriage relationships, don't succeed. We constantly do things wrong, backward, or 180 degrees out of phase with the way GOD would want it done. The sad thing is we do it that way because that is what everybody does. We follow that failing model even though we can see the poor results that everybody gets.

There used to be a process that preceded dating called courting. Courting was the edification or examination process that was used to see if a person would be good to marry. The second step in that edification process would move a couple into developing intimacy. Contrary to popular belief intimacy is obtained through talking not intercourse. This is where the phrase "talking to" came into play in reference to dating, i.e., "Rick is talking to Sharon or Rick and Sharon are talking". The intimacy phase of courting is where the couple would delve into each other's personality, mentally and emotionally, to gain an understanding who the person really is at the core level of their being. The intimacy phase is where I can find out if the person I want to marry is really in-to-me-see. Any woman who has sex with a man before she obtains intimacy or before she understands who he really is sets herself (and the children she might have with him) up for failure. If she becomes pregnant, she is going to reproduce after his kind. Whatever he has living in him will be reproduced through her.

Courting is a process where we strip away all of the pretence so that we can see who the person really is and intelligently decide if marrying this person makes sense. We are not supposed begin dating a person until after we have gone to this intimate level with them and are confident that we really know who they really are. Once you feel this person would be good to marry because you know them intimately then a couple should make a commitment to marriage and set a wedding date. This is the point where dating should begin.

Now, this is also where the term "going together" used to apply (once upon a time) in reference to dating. Again, the only place two people should be "going together" is to the altar. The purpose of going together is to fulfill the commitment they made to get married on a specified date. No one should ever claim to be "going with" someone when they have not made a commitment to go anywhere permanent with their relationship. A more appropriate term would be "playing with" rather than going with.

Once a couple has obtained intimacy and began dating, their "talking" must now move into the conversation phase. Their conversation must begin being directed more towards planning the marriage. That is, how the two of them are going to become one. The purpose of conversation is to cause conversion so that the couple comes into agreement. That is, to convert one to the other's way of thinking on every matter pertaining to marriage. This conversation or conversion process is designed to establish what the vision for the couple's marriage will be, how the marriage will function, what they will do, and what they hope to achieve by becoming married. Once they are both in agreement, then they can go to the altar on the DATE they set.

All of this sounds very hard and too much to go through to get married. However, most marriages end in divorce precisely because couples don't want to go through the tough process of discovering if a person would be right to marry. We want dating to be easy in the microwave society. But dating was always meant to be hard. In reality, it should be hard for a man to get a woman to commit to marry him who she does not really know. It should be hard to get a woman to have sex with a man who she is not married to. However, in 2011, it is waaaay too easy.

Securing happiness in marriage is not a matter of finding the right person. It is a matter of being the right person. You cannot have the right person for you until after you become the right person for someone else! If you are not right for the person you want to marry, he or she is also not the right person for you. No matter how good they look or how desirable they are if they are not right for you they will not be good to you.

In order to become the right person for someone to marry, you must first be single. That is, whole within yourself and connected and one with GOD. Both parties must be whole or single because two half people will make a whole mess. To become the right person for someone else, you must be committed to becoming one with them and you must understand the difference between being committed and being involved. When you look at a ham and egg breakfast you can clearly see that the chicken was only involved in making the breakfast whereas the pig was committed. The chicken just laid a few eggs and kept living but the pig had to die to make that breakfast possible. When you are committed to being married, you must actually die to your single life.

If you want a real fulfilling marriage relationship it requires work and there must be great sacrifice. The more you want the relationship the greater the sacrifice you must put forth. If you have a person in your life that you really like and it does not appear that they are putting forth any real sacrifice to have a relationship with you, you need to stop and direct your time and energy elsewhere. Eventually you are going to have a problem with them either looking to leave or demanding compensation for your occupation of their time. Ladies, the person who you will want to be your boo is the person who is diligently seeking to marry you.

Hebrews 11:6 says "He that comes to GOD must believe that HE is and that HE rewards those who diligently seek HIM." You were made in the image and likeness of GOD so whatever is good for GOD is good for you too. Therefore, anyone who wants to marry you must believe that you "is" the one for them and that you will reward him who diligently seeks you. Proverbs 18:22 says "He who finds a wife finds a good, and obtains favor of the Lord." If a person does not diligently seek to marry you, they should not receive favor or a reward of sex and service. A person who is diligently seeking your hand in marriage will sacrifice their time, energy, effort, and even money to pursue and marry you.

Diligently seeking you is not obsession, it is hot pursuit. Seeking diligently someone is not stalking. It is an effectual, fervent pursuit of your time, attention, and affection. James chapter 5 says the fervent effectual prayer of the righteous man avails much or makes much available. When someone who is righteous, fervent, and effectual comes after you, it should make you want to

Relationships

make much of your time and energy available to them permanently.

Now, a person who is diligently seeking you has moved mentally from the belief level of relationship to faith. They must believe or have come to the conclusion that you "is" the one for them and have moved in their mind to the faith level. They have grown to the point where they are ready to move to the level of knowing, to learn what pleases you, so that they can receive the reward. The reward that you give at this stage of the relationship is not your body. You reward them with your time, attention, and perhaps affection in order to see if they will truly be good for you not just good to you.

Whenever you are really sold out to the fact that you want to marry a specific person, you must get to know who they are at their inner being. The main two things that you want to know comes from Philippians 3:10. You will want to know who that person in the power of his or her resurrection and in the fellowship of their suffering.

Resurrection means to come back to life or to make a decision to live. You see, almost everyone has been through something that made them feel like they wanted to die or made them want to just give up. You will want to know what power they used or where they found the strength to hold on to or come back to life. That is the power of their resurrection. The other thing you want to know about a person is the fellowship of their suffering. What are the trials and tribulations that he or she has been through, how they handled them, and what they learned as a result? This will not only give you knowledge of what they have endured but also a look into their character to see if they have integrity. That is, their ability to remain one with GOD even while it appears they are under tremendous pressure from GOD. This will give you a preview of how they will perform when they have to endure tough times with you.

When someone is really interested in marrying you, they will try to get to know you. If you are asking all of the questions and seeking knowledge of them and they don't appear to be interested in knowing you, don't waste your time and energy with them. Now, the knowledge I am referring to has nothing to do with finding out your sign, where you work, go to school, or what kind of CDs you like. That type of knowledge is superficial. A person who is really interested in knowing you and not just gaining access to your body will want to obtain intimate knowledge of who you are, what you like and don't like, the things that please, excite, and motivate you; the things that make you feel good, loved, and cared for apart from intercourse. These are the types of things that a person would want to know who is really interested in having a long lasting relationship with you.

Now, a man will be interested in pursuing a marriage

relationship with a woman whereas a man sized boy will only be interested in going to bed with her. A man will want to get into a woman's mind whereas a boy will want to get into her behind. You will know if a man sized male is really a boy or a man by whether he pursues your mind or your behind. The man sized boy is dangerous because he suffers from a psychological condition known as arrested development. He has a man sized body but the mind of a 12 year old adolescent. When a man sized boy cannot get what he wants, he will throw a temper tantrum like a little boy. However, because he is man sized he is too powerful. Once he becomes overly emotional, he can do great damage very quickly. A woman will never be able to please or control him all the time. When he can't get his way he may destroy something or destroy her because of it. So a woman must be sure that the male she is interested in is a man and not just man sized.

Finally, both men and women have to learn to communicate with each other. However, women must be able to articulate to men more clearly (that means in fewer words) what they want and need them to provide. Different women want and need different things, so don't let a man treat you like the last chick he was with. Make it a point to tell him what you want and need from the relationship and make sure that he is listening. Don't wait until he is watching the game on TV to decide to have this conversation. Do it while you are having a meal or sharing quiet time together. Then, you must also get him to express to you exactly what he wants and needs from you.

Now, men, while each woman has different wants and needs, every woman has the same basic wants and needs. Although they have these wants and needs, they find it hard to express exactly what they are so that most men can understand.Men, we have to be taught or led to understand that every woman wants attention, affection, and intimacy. Attention is gained for a woman when you stop whatever you are doing and focus on her. Affection is demonstrated when you touch her at times other than when you want sex. Intimacy occurs when you talk to her, share your thoughts, and listen to hers. The keys to providing a woman with attention, affection, and intimacy is by stopping for her, talking to her, and touching her.

Every woman needs security. There are three specific types of security that she needs: Physical, financial, and emotional. She must have all three of these needs provided not just one or two. A man might be the greatest man on the planet in providing two of these needs. However, if one of them is missing, there is going to be a problem because a need is not being met.

I sometimes receive much flack from feminist women when I say that even grown, independent, professional women are attracted to or like to have a man who can make them feel safe. Too many women in the professional category say they don't need a man for anything. On the other hand, they will admit that they would like to have a committed relationship with a good man. They want a man who is sensitive to their needs but they also want their man to be a real man's man. The issue here beyond the feminist rhetoric really boils down to satisfying a primary need. That need is a need for security; more specifically physical security.

A woman may not be looking for a man who is always fighting in the street but she does want to know that her man can fight if he has to. If they were attacked on the street, she wouldn't want her man to make a squeezed doll sound as he pulls her in front of him. If there is a noise when they are in bed at night, she would want him to get up and check. Although she can do the same job as a man can in the business world, she still wouldn't want a man who might hide in the closet or suggest that she go to see if someone is out there. Even with all of the paying the bills, being led by GOD, and so on, going on that some women say they want in a man, not being able or willing to provide physical security would be a complete turn off to all of them. The average woman, no matter how strong and tough she is, wants a man who she knows can protect her if he has to. The examples I cited here are things that have actually happened to women that I know. The experience of discovering they did not have a protector in the man they were with caused some of them to turn to the bad-boy. They could satisfy most of their own primary needs so they choose to be with a male who can provide physical security although they knew that he may not really be a real man mentally and emotionally.

Now, men, every woman also needs financial security. If you hear a woman say that she doesn't need financial security from a man, it's crap. Don't pay any attention to her because if you are not holding up your end financially, she is going to start looking for another dude. Financial security is a primary need that must be fulfilled. A woman feels financially secure when the bills are paid, her children have food and clothes, and she has the things that she needs to be comfortable in her home.

Financial security is a very big area for a woman. Bad finances can kill a marriage quicker than adultery. A woman might forgive a man for sleeping with another woman because she knows how other women are. That old heifer might have tricked her man anyway. But, don't let her get evicted because the rent was not paid. Or don't let the light, gas, or cable get cut off. And you'd better not let the kids have to go without food or wear tattered old clothes. She is not going to tolerate that at all.

The last need that every woman has, my brothers, is emotional security. A woman feels emotionally secure when her man simply responds to her needs. Whenever you hear your woman say the words "I need", you have to drop whatever you are doing and respond immediately. It might be something simple like "I need you to take out the trash". When she comes to ask you to take out the trash, in her mind she is thinking that you should have recognized that it needed to be taken out. Therefore, while she might ask you nicely, she is actually having an emotional reaction to the trash being in the house and she wants it out… now! You will provide her with emotional security when you drop whatever you are doing and respond to her emotional needs immediately. If you wait to do it later, her emotional need will not be satisfied. You may as well not do it at all. She needs an immediate response in these situations in order to feel emotionally secure.

The basics of building love successfully requires you to obtain knowledge about who you are and the person that you want to be in love with. Anyone who does not understand the purpose of a man, woman, child, relationship, or any other thing, is going to misuse or abuse those things. Therefore, if you desire to build a strong relationship or marriage, you must obtain the knowledge you need to do it right and to get it right the first time.

Chapter 4
PREPARE TO CHANGE

"Consider how hard it is to change yourself and you'll understand what little chance you have in trying to change others." ~ William Shakespeare

One of the chief struggles that couples have in a marriage or relationship is with change. I have heard some people complain that their mate is trying to change them and go on to explain how they are resisting that change. The bible says in Hosea 4:6 "My people are destroyed for a lack of knowledge." I find that many marriages are destroyed for the same reason. They do not know why change is absolutely necessary in order for a marriage to be successful. My guess is if they knew better, they would do better. The people who resist change in marriage do not know that there are two main reasons why their spouse is trying to get them to change.

The first reason why some people try to change their spouse is to transform them into the type of person that they wanted rather than enjoying the person they picked. When those resisting change in a relationship get a sense that this may be the reason their mate is insisting upon change, they have a decision to make as to whether or not to remain in that relationship.

Relationships

If the person insisting on change does not realize that he or she is not married to the right person, that relationship could turn abusive. Sit them down and try to get a clear understanding, without arguing, of why your spouse feels it is necessary for you to change. If you don't get a sense that their reason for insisting that you change is healthy, then you should consider leaving.

The second reason a person will be insisting upon change is because change is an essential element of becoming married and creating compatibility. You see, there is a difference between getting married and being married. Getting married is a one day event whereas being married is a process that takes three to five years to complete depending on the couple's willingness to change. The longer it takes them to change from being single the longer it will take for them to convert to being married.

Getting married is easy. Anybody can get married but not everybody can be married. The process of being or becoming married is like making mashed potatoes. The couple must first have the skin of pride and selfishness stripped off of them so that they can become spiritually, physically, and emotionally naked before one another. Then they must be cut up into small pieces, immersed in water or the word of GOD, and then exposed to the heat (or pressure) of the marriage process until they become soft, pliable or conformable. The couple will no longer be two individual potatoes at this point. They will appear to be one but the process of being married is not complete. Next, they must be mashed, beat, or whipped by a metal instrument, the sword of the spirit of GOD, until they are completely folded into one another.

Now the two individuals have completely become one at this point or actually married. Here, you can add butter and cream to the mix to make the marriage rich and sweet or salt and pepper to spice it up. The marriage process fails when the two individuals start the process of being mashed together but refuse to be stripped of their individuality first. Rather than growing to the point of being married where their relationship is a smooth, rich, and spicy mix, they only end up beat up. There is a difference between a mashed potato and a smashed potato.

Both parties in a relationship have to make changes initially and adjustments periodically to keep their marriage in compatibility. Whenever you go before an altar to get married it should be readily apparent that change is going to be required. The word alter, whether you spell it with an e or an a means to change. Two people going before an altar to must alter their minds from thinking like a single person to thinking like a married couple. They must change. All of the thoughts that they had about shopping, socializing, even sleeping, and so on, have to change from providing for one to taking care of two. Couples who have difficulty making this transition of thought and those who fuss or argue throughout the process are said to be "going through changes".

Persons preparing to go before an altar to get married must realize that it will require them to go through 8 processes in order for them to be married and remain married. For couples who choose to fuss and argue those processes will be very difficult to get through. Those processes are: change, sacrifice, service, exposure, redefined, pressure, endurance, and fulfillment.

Change – a couple must first recognize the difference between getting married and being married. Being married is a mental and physical condition. Everyone who gets married does not realize that they must set a goal to change from being single to being married. Couples that want to be married must be willing to change their minds and ways from being single to being married in order to remain married after getting married.

Sacrifice – a married person must eliminate their connection to most of the people, places, activities, and things associated with their single life in order to make a successful transition into married life. The longer they take to cut their connections to being single the longer it will take to be married.

Service – married couples must be willing to serve one another in sickness and health, in riches and poverty, in good times and bad, and until death. Proper service requires communication and agreement because you have to know what to do, how to do it, and when to do it in order to satisfy the person being served. There is nothing worse than getting bad service. Service to each other will lead to the recognition of the vision or mission that GOD had in mind for putting you two together. Proper service to each other will lead you to obtain the wealth that GOD meant for your family to have. Every couple gets a dowry from GOD but its release is connected to the execution of the couple's GOD given vision or mission.

Exposure – a married person can no longer hide their personal secrets. Whatever was done in the dark shall come to light and at the most inopportune times. Therefore a person who wants to be married must confess and reveal who they are or what they are hiding because their spouse is going to eventually find out.

Redefined – who you are as a single person is not who you will be as a married person. You will be transformed much like a caterpillar is transformed into a butterfly. Therefore, what you are called and how you are viewed must be redefined. When Robert Smith marries Katherine Jones they are now redefined as Mr. and Mrs. Robert Smith. He is no longer to be defined as just him; he is they. She is no longer to be defined as Katherine Jones, she is Mrs. Robert Smith. Everything that is assigned to his name now defines her and vice versa. In Genesis chapter

Relationships

5 verse 1, you will find that before the fall Adam and Eve were both called Adam. She received a different name after they both defied the order of GOD. Becoming redefined will keep a couple living in line with the order of GOD for their family. It will cause your spouse to grow to believe in you and gain a growing sense of what you really believe in or stand for. That will make it easier for them to submit to being one with you.

Pressure – the weight of mental constraint will become heavy as you recognize that you must renew your mind from being single to being married. You can no longer think like a single person; only of yourself. Once you ate dinner as a single person, your whole family was fed. Now you have to make sure your spouse has had their dinner as well. Your thoughts must really only be concerned with the care and comfort of your spouse. But there will be mental and emotional pressure arising from periodic conflicts that you will have with your spouse as you make the transition from selfishness to selflessness. Your own mind will try to pressure you to conclude that it is too hard to care for someone else and that you will be better off being single again. The biggest fight that you will have in the pressure process is with yourself.

Endurance – enduring the pressure of the process of renewing your mind will lead to you and your spouse having one heart and one mind. Enduring until the end of the pressure process will totally relieve the pressure and prepare you to prosper. A piece of cheap coal has to endure intense pressure in order to become an expensive diamond. The pressure process will cause the two of you to press into each other and become one which will make you more valuable than two. This pressure is like being trapped in a very tight space together. You move and adjust your position in this space until both of you are comfortable. Now you can endure for a long time in a confined space when you work together as one. The longer you endure the pressure of confinement, and make your primary concern your spouse's comfort, the quicker you will adjust to becoming one. Once the two of you move into each other mentally, the area of confinement will seem to increase, thus, relieving the pressure emotionally. Completing this process gives you credibility with your mate which leads to trust in the relationship.

Fulfillment – after you and your spouse have made the transition into being married the fulfillment process begins. Now, you can begin to pursue purpose. At some point passion will wear off and the two of you will settle into purpose. Purpose means to fulfill the mission that GOD put you together to complete. As you begin to work to fulfill your divine purpose, you will begin to realize that you cannot do it without each other. When you were single you believed that you could do or be anything that you put your mind to. Now, you will recognize that you cannot do or be what you want to do or be without your spouse. Thus, you will learn to love him or her as you

Relationships

love yourself. Fulfillment of your purpose as a couple will lead to personal or individual fulfillment as well.

What is the conclusion of the matter as it relates to change in a relationship? Life is comprised of a series of changes that begin at the moment of conception. We change from a zygote to an embryo; from a baby to an adult; from adult to elderly. The sky constantly changes from dark to light as day turns to night. Yesterday turns into today and the New Year turns into next year. The one constant in the world is change but the one process that humans most stubbornly resist is change.

In order for a caterpillar to become a butterfly it must submit to the process of change. In order for the caterpillar to change into a butterfly it had to be willing to sacrifice its life as a caterpillar, and endure the pressure of being alone in a tight cocoon. Tribulation always precedes transformation and elevation. The pattern of change in life appears to be that we must go down before we can go up. This makes life like a toaster: you have to go down and be transformed in the heat of tribulation before you can "pop up" or be elevated at the set time. A caterpillar is the lower level of life for a butterfly. It had to be willing to be entombed in a tight cocoon and die to its former life in order for it to transform into what it was created to be. Similarly, couples have to submit to the process of going down together, and dying to their single life, so they can arise as one or something different than they were before.

WHY IS IT HARD TO GET MARRIED?

As I stated previously, there is a difference between getting married and being married. Men and women in today's society are having great difficulty growing to the point where they qualify emotionally and intellectually to get married. An unwillingness to change knowledge, attitudes, myths, and misconceptions that they have come to believe about the opposite sex, and marriage in general, is causing a high level of fear, apprehension and tension between the sexes. Fear comes as a result of a lack of knowledge. Just as fear and a lack of knowledge produce racism and prejudice among the races, a lack of knowledge and operating on false knowledge also creates fear and separation between the sexes. In order to change the current conditions, we must first change our minds. We must purge ourselves of the prejudices, preconceived notions, and stereotypes that we hold about the opposite sex. Those of us who want to be married must also change the way we see ourselves and our general attitude about sex and marriage.

One would expect the opposite to be true but unmarried people in the professional class find it harder to get married than those in the blue collar class. It is because of their degrees and the social dribble they ascribe to from radio and TV that makes them believe they have the knowledge they need to succeed in a relationship. Yet, it appears to be

Relationships

more difficult for them to find someone with whom they can form the perfect union. It is tougher for them because they don't want to change. I hate to make it seem that I am in the habit of targeting blacks for observation, analysis, and/or criticism but of all the races in America African Americans have the biggest problem in this area.

The following information is an analysis of the state of marriage in America. It is snapshot of the tribulations that all races experience as a whole. I am primarily directing my comments toward the African American condition because statistically they have the greatest problem with obtaining and maintaining happy marriages. They need 911 emergency assistance to help them understand how to get together and stay together more than any other group. One of the reasons this is occurring with African Americans is due to a lack of knowledge and a refusal to give up old untrue knowledge, negative attitudes, and gender bias beliefs.

The US Census Bureau statistics reveals that in 1940, 95% of African Americans with children were married. In 1960 that figure dropped to 70% and in 2006 it declined further to 35%. This means that only 35% of black children live in two parent households compared to 70% of white children. Out of wedlock births escalated from 25% in 1960 to nearly 73% in 2008 for all black children and from 3% to 28% respectively for white children.

Sociologist Andrew J. Cherlin revealed that a black child was more likely to grow up living with both parents during slavery days than he or she is today. Black women were also more likely to be married as a slave than they are today. Most people attempt to look at this condition and conclude that it is the result of a complex set of issues that is an extension of 400 years of slavery and Jim Crow oppression. However, I contend that the problem can be solved almost instantaneously if we were just willing to do one thing: change.

The debate over relationship issues in magazines, on TV, and radio often center on the black professional. The average person cannot seem to understand why women who appear to be blessed with talent, brains, and beauty are having difficulty finding someone to marry. Then the debate will eventually breakdown to the question of whether or not some women's standards are too high or if there is just a lack of available men for these women to choose from?

The answer is actually both in the social context but, as I said, it is not the answer that will correct the problem. Taking a look at the problem from the social context, the US Census shows that there are 1.8 million more black women in America than black men. Out of the total black male population only 54% of black men are available for black professional women to choose to marry. Their eligibility and availability are limited as a result of a high rate of incarceration, a lack of employment, and little to no education. There are still a high percentage of good black men in America, who work hard every day, that have no high school diploma. However, black professional women are reluctant to select from this pool of men because the black feminist intelligencer constantly proffers the unproven theory that they are going to have problems if they marry one of these men.

The question is then presented to further the debate: Should black professional women just pick a man to marry in an effort to create a stable family and begin the process of rebuilding a dying community? Or should they wait until they can find a man who meets their "standards" and have it all while taking on the responsibility of rebuilding the black family and community? The problem with these debates is they provide NO clear action upon which to solve the problem or create the requisite change. What the debate does do, however, is deepen the level of divisive discourse between the sexes. They can't agree on what the problem is therefore they can't move from where they are to begin to fix it. At the end of the debate, which usually becomes heated, men and women actually move further apart as they separate into their neutral corners. The debate often leads many women to conclude that men who work but do not earn a lot of money or have a degree are ineligible for them to marry.

I had an employee once whom I discovered looked

down on her dad. He was only a janitor, to quote her, while her mother was a Registered Nurse. This young lady had a Bachelor Degree. I asked her if her father lived in the home and raised her from a child to which she answered yes. I then asked if her father's salary helped to pay for her college education to which she also replied yes. His labor helped to get her where she needed to be but somehow she developed an attitude that allowed her to look down on her father simply because of his profession. She loved her dad but his profession, the fruits of which she enjoyed, was not respectable in her sight. Actually, she did not see him as being a professional. Sadly, I had to inform her that anything anyone does on a daily basis that they get paid for regularly is a profession. It may "only" be in janitorial engineering, but it is a profession nonetheless. It is said that a girl will marry a man who reminds her of her father. However, it was clear to me that if this young lady found a guy who was just like her dad, but he was also a janitor, she would not choose him to marry.

One of the reasons professional women are finding it hard to marry is because many have come to believe through rhetoric from radio, TV, movies, and magazines that what a man earns should weigh heavily in the decision on whom they choose to marry. On the contrary, a woman's selection should be based on who he is not what he earns or what he does. As one woman said, in an ABC News interview on this topic "If it weren't for the intangibles, the allure of the lovey-dovey stuff, I wouldn't have gotten married. The benefits of marriage are his character and his caring. If not for that, why bother?"

Most single women that I know (from all races) over the age of 30 would not mind getting married. But they believe that the type of man they want and the quality of marriage they would need may not be likely. They also believe it would be "settling" to simply marry a man that doesn't meet their "standards".So they find themselves torn between two conditions which leave them frozen and unable to make a profitable decision that would satisfy their desires.

To further complicate matters, many women have become concerned that if they make more money than their husband it will lead to divorce. According to a study by Jay Teachman, a sociologist at Western Washington University, published in the October 2010 issue of the Journal of Family Issues, A married couple is only 38% percent more likely to divorce when the wife earns more than the husband. However, out of the 2,500 women who participated in the study that result was only true when the woman was bringing in 60% or more of the household income. Statistically, this disproves the commonly held belief that ALL marriages in which the wife earns more are more likely to end in divorce. The rate of divorce for women in this category is only 38% compared to the overall rate of 53%.

Now, professional men are heavily contributing to the problem as well. They are often reluctant to make a commitment to marry professional women. Many professional women who have a college degree, a job, own a home, and drive a nice car, seem to believe that these things make them a great catch. However, many men, professional or otherwise, don't see it that way. Many professional men see the professional woman as a financial liability. They ask in conversations amongst themselves, how many beautiful professional women still owe multiple 10s or 100s of thousands on a student loan? Yes, she may own a house but is it paid for? How many 10s or 100s of thousands does she still owe on it? How much debt is she carrying on credit cards from her pursuit of a profession and the trappings of having to dress professionally, including driving a luxury car with a large note, will she bring into a marital union?

Many professional men believe the professional woman could potentially be a heavy financial bag which she is going to want him to help her with if not completely carry. Professional men are also becoming increasingly concerned that women who have a pretty face and a nice body don't feel the need to develop character and other qualities. It appears that this type of woman holds the expectation that a man is supposed accept them as they are, shower them with gifts when they are dating, and take care of them financially when they are married. Professional men are afraid of being ruined financially therefore they are putting off marriage entirely. Professional men want a woman who can bring something to the table immediately, who is virtually debt free, and who won't end up being a financial liability.

Some professional men also complain that it seems women want men to overlook their baggage while at the same time they are not willing to overlook the man's baggage, such as a child out of wedlock. They want him to put up with all of their stuff while being unwilling to be patient with them as they deal with their child's mother. Men are beginning to express concern that if a woman has had bad experiences with men prior to him, like not having a father, she is carrying some emotional baggage that she is going to unpack during their marriage. They know that they are going to have to deal with whatever is in those bags. The fear is, if they do not know how to deal with that baggage and are not able to get her to either drop the bag or unpack it successfully, it could cost them dearly financially once they divorce. They know that she will end up walking away with all of her money and half of his. Marriage is a great financial risk for men today.

For this and many other reasons highly educated and/or wealthy black men tend to "out marry" or marry outside their race at a higher rate than black women. Professional black men want a woman who not only has money but also knows how to manage money and is not already strapped with a lot of debt. This is an opportunity or luxury that black men seem to have. Black women, on the other hand, are either much more reluctant to marry outside their race or do not have the opportunity to do so. A sociological line of inquiry called the "exchange theory" suggests that in the piggy bank of goods that each of us bring to a relationship — money, smarts, sense of humor, looks, family background, education, gender — African heritage is devalued compared with European or Asian heritage. African-American females, even with lots of education, are not perceived to have as much "value" in the marriage market. That may be a cold way to look at love, romance, and sex, but studies dating back to the 1980s support it.

Now, statistically, black women have increasingly had success in marrying wealthy white men over the last 10 years at a rate that has doubled over the previous 10 years. But those couples still find great difficulty when the black bride is taken home to old moneyed mommy. A sister finds out quickly that the devil does wear Prada! The bad news for black men who marry white women is interracial couples tend to have higher rates of divorce primarily due to family pressures and influences. Divorce is equivalent to financial murder for men because the courts often give more than half of their earnings to their ex-wife especially when children are involved.

Now, what I am about to share may get me in real trouble. Oprah might personally chop off my head and let the people at Harpo play soccer with it. I am a straight-up fan of Oprah so I watch her nearly every day. If she had ever gotten in to trouble, I would have made a crying video like that guy did with Brittney Spears: "Leave Oprah alone!" I love Whitney Houston too so when it was announced that Oprah was going to interview her I cleared my schedule. I had to be there to see every minute of it.

As I listened to Whitney talk about her relationship with Bobby Brown she confirmed what I always suspected: Bobby had a problem being Mr. Houston! Whitney could not be all that she could be and remain married to Bobby because her career far outshined his. Thus she crowned him the king of pop in an effort to raise him up. The combination of pride and ego however made him, either consciously or unconsciously, hold her back from going as far as she could go. Her movie and music career was on an incredible rise when she met him but ended up in a terrible low. Like many women who decide to stay with a cheating husband she resorted to using substances to soothe her broken heart. Their example proves, ladies, how the wrong man can powerfully damage the prospects of a good woman.

As I watched the interview I could see that Oprah totally related to what Whitney was saying relative to Bobby not being able to handle her success. In all of the interviews I've seen Oprah do I have never seen her eyes light up and appear to be almost captivated as Whitney told her story. When Whitney said "A man has got to have his own" Oprah said "ummmm" and I could see that she really felt that. Usually when a woman can strongly relate to another woman's story like that it's because she either has had or is having a similar experience. It could be (and you know that I don't really know if this is true which is why she might kill me) Oprah may be having similar problems with Stedman.

The look in her eyes said to me that Stedman may not treat her as well as she wants to be treated and may cause her to experience some emotional turmoil. I am probably totally wrong. But because I have seen this before I know, and I suspect you know also, that this can happen when a successful woman (who is well over the 60% income comparison threshold) is with a man who is not as successful. Now, to be clear, this really has nothing to do with the money that the woman makes as it is more often about the pride in the man's heart. It's the man not the money that makes the difference.

Some guys can totally handle their wife making more money and having greater celebrity than they do. (Oh, GOD, I just realized that I may have to hide from Stedman too. They may both jump me on the street) On the other hand, some guys because of their pride must have other women to make them FEEL good. At the same time, they keep women like Oprah and Whitney felling bad.

Stedman appears to be holding his own with his books

and speaking engagements. However, sometimes guys in his position, although he really loves Oprah, do not want to be Mr. Winfrey. Sometimes it is not the money it's the man. You see, let me be Mr. Winfrey! Give me half a chance to be Mr. Houston or Mr. Berry! Oprah would not just be the richest black woman in America she would end up being the richest person in the world. Whitney would actually hit those high notes again. Halle would own Hollywood. Some men just know how to maximize another person's potential. Like football coaches they can motivate a person to perform beyond their own vision of themselves. We see a lot of Halley's external beauty, for example, but the right "coach" can help her to radiate her inner beauty, creativity, and leadership ability. Halley is at the point of her career where she should begin to consider owning her own studio. The right life partner could help her get there.

Having said this I can hear the feminists now: "A woman don't need a man to become what she wants to be!" That is true. She may not "need" a man to help her but having a good man in her corner would sure make it easier. GOD did not design us as human beings to be alone. HE said, "It's not good for man (or woman) to be alone." Life is easier in every area when we have a good partner to help us get to where we want to be, support us in the effort, and cheer us on when we reach the rough places. Two people with the same heart and mind, working together, will always achieve more than one person working alone. A man, if nothing else, needs a warm, soft, loving place to lay his head at the end of a hard day. A woman is a caring being that has to be cared for in order bring out the best that she has in her. While a woman can go out into the ring of the business world and fight, just like a man, she still needs to have a good "second" or someone in her corner. No boxer, no matter how good or talented, can win at a high level without having someone in their corner. She needs to have a strong pair of arms to rest in and hold her sometimes. Whether we'd like to admit it or not we all need the support of others. It somehow propels us to higher levels when that person is the same person that we are in love with.

On the other hand, it seems to stifle our creativity and capacity for productivity when we do not receive the support that we should from the person we love. The main reason I believe this support does not come forth is primarily due to pride but secondarily is the result of a lack of knowledge. Some men just don't know what to do to make their wife's creativity and productivity come through. I believe the single major factor that causes the majority of marriages to end is a lack of knowledge.

We all know how to get married but most of us were never taught how to BE married. As a result of not having knowledge on how to BE married, we tend to operate off clichés such as a marriage should be 50/50. However, 50% is a failing grade! Marriage should be 100/100 with both partners bringing a 100% effort to the marriage. They must both apply 100% effort in order to produce children that will contribute 100% of their talents to the development of their country, economy and community. We expect our children to produce a 100% effort in school but how can they be motivated to do that consistently when they see their parents only putting forth a 50% effort at home. A lack of knowledge on how to BE married makes it difficult to remain married. That is especially true if we were divorced and didn't learn what WE did wrong in the previous marriage. A lack of knowledge on what we need to change from the way we operated in the old marriage will lead to separation or divorce in the new marriage.

CHANGE: A REVOLUTION OF U!

"Revolution is an extension of evolution. Evolution is a gradual change in the nature of a thing that over a long period of time leads to revolution, which is quick change." – Dick Gregory

Everyone knows that there are changes that we need to make about and within ourselves which is the reason why we make New Year's resolutions annually. Each year we vow to do that one thing that we believe is going to change our lives, improve our lives, or make us happier. Yet, when it comes to marriage and relationships we seem to focus on the changes that our partner needs to make. We believe that we would be happy if they would just... In this regard we must understand that happiness is not a condition it is a choice. We make ourselves unhappy because of the way we choose to view whatever our partner may do that is unpleasing. If we resolve to change the way that we allow the little things that occur in a relationship to drive us nuts, we can become happy by simply letting our partner be. This would require a sort of revolution of the heart and mind to discover and destroy that thing within us that makes some little thing that our partner does devastatingly irritating. I know a couple who had been together 30 years that was about to break up over unfilled ice trays. The partner that it bothered terribly realized that they needed to just stop allowing it to bother them and that stopping had to be continuous. It couldn't be achieved as a resolution, there had to be a revolution in their heart and mind in order for the couple to be happy again.

Have you ever wondered by resolutions don't work? A resolution is doomed to fail because repetition is inherent in the nature of a resolution. A resolution is a Re Solution. Re = over again. So a RE-solution is a solution to a problem that must be actively applied over and over again. It's no wonder then why we make the same resolutions every year, fail to achieve the desired solution, and end up having to apply the same solution over again the next year. It is time that we grow to the point where we say: No more resolutions. We have long been resolving to make that change which would lead us to happiness, fortune, or fame but each year we come up lame. We have long been preparing to change. It's time now for quick change. It's time now to get ready for the true revolution u!

A "volution" (I know that I'm making up a word. It is actually spelled volition) is the act or an instance of "u" making a conscious choice or decision to turn or move in a new direction. A RE volUtion, then, is the act or decision that you or I must make repeatedly to turn and keep moving in a new direction. It is a willful act of committing and recommitting repetitiously as we move purposefully toward our destiny. The roads we travel as we drive to our destinations are never perfectly straight so we must make many minor adjustments with the steering wheel in order to remain on course. There are obstacles in the road at times that make us veer off course. But our volution of mind REdirects us back in line and motivates us to redeem the lost time.

"The future is not a result of choices among alternative paths offered by the present, but a place that is created first in the mind and will, created next in activity. The future is not some place we are going to, but one we are creating. The paths to our destinies are not to be found, but made, and the activity of making them changes both the maker and the destination." - John Schaar

Is it possible to create a new person or new path by utilizing an old process or following old directions? If the solution, the act or process that we apply to solve an old problem, does not solve the problem, is that really a solution? Any solution that must be applied over and over again is just a temporary fix. A real solution should relieve the problem permanently. Dieting, for example, is a temporary fix because we must diet perpetually in order to keep the weight off. A volition to make a permanent change in the way U eat, what U eat, when U eat, along with increasing physical activity, and will provide a permanent solution to a weight problem and bring about a revolUtion.

A sol-U-tion is actually an act or instance of determining what is required to solve or figure out how to become the U that you were meant to be. George Eliot said "It is never too late to become what you might have been." The $64,000 question is when will you change? You know that you need to change. You know the resolutions you have made in past years to become the U that you want to be haven't worked.
So, the question is when will you really change and what will be the catalyst for that change?

"Some people change when they see the light, others when they feel the heat." - Caroline Schoeder

A change, revolution, in the way we see ourselves will help us to become what we really want to be. If I dream of myself as being fat, I will always be fat. However, if I begin to see myself as a man with ripped muscles and a

Relationships

six-pack that is what I will become. As Mahatma Gandhi said "You must be the change you wish to see in the world." The change we want to see in our body, we must first be in our mind. So I have to already BE the change, mentally and spiritually, that I want to see physically. The solution only requires a little change but it demands quick change; a revolution not an evolution. A revolutionary change cannot be made utilizing a resolutionary process.

There is a difference between a movement and a revolution. Inherent in the nature of a movement is the fact that at some point it will stop. You will find that is true in social or political movements, musical movements, and even bowel movements. At some point the movement will end and we will start to slowly return to the point where we began. Revolution, on the other hand, creates movement in the desired direction that never stops. By making resolutions we allow ourselves to get lulled into the slow transformation trap and get pulled back into our old ways and habits over time.Life is like running on a treadmill. If we don't keep pressing forward, we will begin to roll back. Starting a revolution will bring about an immediate change in our minds (thoughts and visions) and actions.

"The greatest revolution in our generation is that of human beings who, by changing the inner attitudes of their mind, can change the outer aspects of their lives." - William James

In order to make a revolutionary change within ourselves we must revolutionize the three parts of our being: body, mind, and spirit; forsaking not the assembly of ourselves together in unity. Our body, mind, and spirit must be in one accord in order to be at peace within ourselves and in union with heaven. This will allow us to actually hear the music of heaven and the voice of GOD. A chord (accord) in music is comprised of three notes in perfect harmony. We come into harmony with GOD, the earth, and the universe when our mind, body, and spirit are in accord or not in conflict. Then we will be able to hear the voice of GOD directing us into the purpose or vision that HE has for our lives. Completing that purpose is our path to wealth.

"Concerning all acts of initiative and creation, there is one elementary truth; that the moment one definitely commits oneself, then Providence moves too." - W.H. Murray

The revolution of our world (marital, physical and financial) begins with a revolution of self. The revolution of the self begins in the mind. Chapter 4 in my book ("Maximizing Fatherhood" that you can find at drwillenterprises.com) entitled "Understanding the Mind" provides critical knowledge needed to complete the revolution of self. Most adults hinder their personal transformation by holding on to childhood traumas. They still see themselves as that hurt little victim. James

Relationships

Hillman said "If you are still being hurt by an event that happened to you at twelve, it is the thought that is hurting you now." Once we understand how the mind works we will be able then to totally revolutionize ourselves. If we let go of limiting thoughts we can become what we know that we were destined to be.

"What is required for effective change is continuity of sincere effort to release and let go of inefficient thought patterns from the past." - Howard Martin

It is time to move away from the past, discard old excuses, eliminate the terrible too's (too young, too poor, too fat, too old, etc.) and decide to move into destiny. Applying a resolution will not let you get there from here. You have probably heard Mariah Carey's "The Transformation of Mimi" (her best selling CD of all time). It's time for you to sing the transformation of me-me. It's time for your personal revolution. No more resolutions. Get ready for the revolution; the revolution of U.

Now, to be clear, there is a difference between the little things that our partner may do to make us unhappy and the big things they may do to derail our future. The only impediment to completing any personal revolution or personal transformation and achievement is one's personal relationships. I have seen women on their way to obtaining a medical degree who ended up with no degree and left saddled alone with several babies. I have seen, and you probably know, young men who had the education, potential, and pedigree to be anything he wanted to be but met the wrong woman and ended up in the penitentiary. Bad relationships can send us spiraling downward into emotional turmoil and could ruin all of our potential. The wrong relationship for me at the wrong time kept me in captivity for two decades financially. It is critically important, then, that we have the right relationships in our lives at the right time. If we are in a relationship that is not good for us, we must decide to revolutionize that relationship by making a permanent change.

This life is actually a dream, like a movie, and you are the director and producer. You can create the scenes of your life and direct it to play out any way you desire. Déjà vu is a scene which occurred in your life that you created in the past and watched unfold in front of your eyes at a later date. Begin to create the scenes of your life and your relationships in your mind today that you want to see in the future. Then do what is necessary to direct the circumstances to produce them. The dream is yours so dream big!

Thoughts always precede action. A journey of a thousand miles does NOT begin with the first step, it begins with the first thought. If we change our way of thinking we will change our way of doing. If we change our way of thinking and doing, we can change our standard of living! Our standard of living is always impacted or influenced by our relationships. When it comes to business we need good relationships with other people. We need contacts to get contracts and a network to get work. Those who always try to go it alone don't usually go very far or they don't go as far as they could have with someone else supporting their efforts and cheering them on. Excellent relationships are key to excellent performance in life, love and in business.

No matter who we are or what we do we must tailor our relationships for the perfect fit. This is critical to keeping our life and relationships stress free and maintaining good productivity. To tailor means to change some things: take some things in, let some things out, or cut some things back. When tailoring relationships for the purpose of achieving goals we must periodic changes. We bring new friends in, let toxic friends go, and cut non-productive associates back. People who are non-productive waste time that could be utilized else wise. Ultimately we have to know where we want to go, do, or be and make the necessary changes in ourselves and our relationships accordingly.

Chapter 5
FORGIVE AND LIVE

"The less you open your heart to others, the more your heart suffers." ~ Deepak Chopra

The Bible shows us that there are many things we are empowered to do when we simply believe only. Trust is the highest level of relationship with GOD wherein we will willingly sacrifice our lives for HIM like Job who said "Though HE slay me yet will I trust HIM". The Bible also reveals that we do not have to get to the level of trust in order to do mighty things with or for HIM. We can heal the sick and raise the dead if we just believe.

Mark 11:22-25 says "...whoever shall say unto a mountain, be removed, or be cast into the sea, and shall not doubt in his heart but believe that those things which he said shall come to pass, he shall have whatsoever he said. Therefore I say to you, whatsoever things that you desire, when you pray, believe that you have already received what you prayed for and you shall have it." Then it says "...when you stand making your request to GOD, forgive your enemies." If we have anything against anybody it is imperative that we forgive them. This way if we forgive whoever we have the power to forgive, GOD will forgive us.

Relationships

Many people have had terrible things done to them by other people in their lives who they trusted. Consequently they have a hard time building trust in all of their relationships and it prevents them from experiencing any long lasting and loving relationship. We need to understand that trust is the highest level of relationship but we can have a good loving relationship with others if we only believe that we can. We can do great things with others and for GOD if we just believe that we can make it happen. Forgiving is hard and is even harder in some situations as compared to others. However, we do not have to punish ourselves for the rest of our lives because some other person hurt us. We do not have to deprive ourselves of the beauty of life and love just because someone did something ugly.

"...if you forgive men their trespasses your heavenly father will also forgive you: But if you forgive not men their trespasses, neither will your Father forgive your trespasses (Matthew 6:14-15)."

Forgiving others not only lets us free ourselves from the prison of past pain it also positions us to be free financially. One of the reasons forgiving others is important is because the universe is designed to release its treasures and blessings only under certain conditions. As we hold unforgiveness in our hearts for another person along with it we hold the hope that the person gets what they deserve and more. We not only want the bad to happen to the person we also wish for the worse that could possibly happen to befall them. Remaining connected to this pain keeps us in poverty or in financial captivity because the universe will not release the best for you while you are wishing the worst for others.

"But love you your enemies and do good and lend hoping for nothing again: and your reward shall be great, and you shall be the children of the Highest: for he is kind to the unthankful and to the evil (Luke 6:35)."

The way that GOD and the universe operates is totally opposite of the way we would operate. The way GOD operates seems to be unfair. Why should I love my enemies especially when they hurt or harmed me and I didn't do a thing to them? GOD is supposed to be on my side. I want HIM to use HIS power to take my enemies out. So why is it that GOD is kind to the evil? The reason GOD operates this way is because GOD is love. Love is the greatest power in the universe. The reason why GOD has not killed satan is because HE still loves him. Sometimes the best way to do away with evil is through love. Sometimes the best way to kill your enemy is through kindness. Forgiving transforms our hearts from hard to soft and allows us to live in the power of love.

Luke chapter 6 not only tells us to love our enemies but it also instructs us to do good to them that hate you, bless them that curse you, and pray for them that spitefully use you. It teaches us to give to every man who asks you for something and don't loan it to him because if he had to ask for a loan, he can't afford to pay it back.

This creates an environment of love in our hearts that allow GOD to trust us to place a great surplus in our hands. GOD gives the surplus to those who have a heart of love so that we can have to distribute when those in real need come to us. You can see that it is important to our future financially to follow the golden rule. Whatever you would want a man to do for you in the same situation you must do for them. If you have anything against anyone, you must forgive them. If you only show love to those that love you, the word says that is not worthy of a reward from heaven because even sinners do that. But if you love your enemies your reward shall be great.

The implication here is that if you do not love your enemies your reward will not be great. But when you give forgiveness it will be given unto you good measure, pressed down, shaken together, and running over will men give forgiveness into your bosom. Unfortunately, most people have been taught erroneously that this lesson pertains to giving money. On the contrary, it is actually a lesson on forgiving. You see, the measure of forgiveness that you give to others will be multiplied and returned back to you. This is why some people have reported going to the bank to pay on their mortgage and discovering that the loan had been forgiven. They now own their home and are debt free because their measure of forgiveness had been multiplied and returned to them in good measure.

Conversely, Jesus gives us the account of a man in Matthew 18 that owed the king a great sum of money. His family was in jeopardy of being sold into slavery if he did not repay what he owed. This man begged the king for forgiveness and the king forgave his debt. This same man then goes out and captures another man who owed him a tiny sum of money. The man begged for forgiveness but he refused to forgive him and commanded that he be thrown into prison until he could repay. The king found out what happened, calls the man in and asked him why he didn't forgive that man in the same manner that he had been forgiven. Being unable to give a proper answer, the king then commanded him to be thrown into prison until he could repay. Jesus gives the moral to the story by saying "so likewise shall my heavenly Father do unto you also if you do not forgive in your hearts everyone of their trespasses".

The reason I shared these biblical examples is to highlight the spiritual, emotional and financial peril that we place ourselves in when we do not forgive those who wronged us in some way. Holding on to hurt effects our health both physically and financially. There is a universal principle that forgiveness is founded on called sowing and reaping. "Whatsoever a man sows that shall he also reap." In America this principle is also expressed as "what goes around comes around." In India they call it karma. No matter where you are in the world and no matter what it is called the principle is still the same. A person will always get back whatever they dish out. However, the return on their giving will always be a multiple of what they gave.

A lack of forgiveness for someone completely who hurt us terribly can cause the death of a marriage or relationship that we want to hold on to desperately. We all know that hurting people tend to hurt other people. When we are carrying around hurt and pain from something that someone has done to us, we have a tendency to pass some of that pain on to those who are closest to us. This can cause us to have difficulty maintaining good relationships with people who we really love because we can't seem to help being mean to them. Refusing to forgive and holding on to the pain caused by someone we hate will cause us to suffer the loss of relationship with those we love.

The real problem here is not so much that the person is suffering from what someone did to them. The bigger problem for the person holding the grudge is the person who they are holding the grudge against probably doesn't even know it and wouldn't even care if he did! He is going on living his life happily, carefree, having already forgiven himself for what he did, and may not even remember anymore that he did it. Yet, the person that he wronged is still holding on to the pain, is suffering the loss of loving relationships, and enduring financial hardships simply because he or she cannot forgive.

I have watched women, especially those that had been raped, having a very hard time maintaining loving relationships due to the trauma of that experience. Too many of them are still suffering from an event that occurred decades ago. Their suffering is also impacting them financially and socially. They had nothing to do with the man attacking them and taking their body. The evil that resides in a man's heart that leads them to hurt someone else was not their problem, it was his problem. But I see too many of women still holding on to the pain of that event and in effect have allowed his problem to become their problem. Not only did the man take their body 10, 20, or 30 years ago, but they have allowed him to steal the joy and happiness of loving relationships from their lives ever since. They have allowed their identity or sense of who they are to become wrapped up in something a sick rapist did to them. They become Jenny "the raped" rather than loving carefree Jenny. Ironically, I see some of these same women in church proclaiming "I'm not gonna let the devil steal my joy" and I think to myself, "really!"

It is crucial their physical, mental, emotional, financial, and social wellbeing that women, especially women who go to church, understand that they are going to have to break the connection they have to their emotional injury. Women who go to church are particularly vulnerable because they think that GOD is going to do it. No, my sister, that is something that you must do. Very few people have the level of faith to cast an evil spirit out of someone who does not want it to come out. That would require a type of exorcism. When a man came to Jesus' disciples to have them cast an evil spirit out of his son they couldn't do it. They asked Jesus why they couldn't do it and he told them it required a level of faith they didn't have (Mark9:17-29).

This affects men too but, again, women are particularly vulnerable to the attachment of evil spirits once they have been sexually abused. The evil spirit works to manipulate and control the host. It controls men in a manner that makes them a predator. It controls women in a manner that makes them prey. The person who molests or sexually abuses someone has an evil spirit that is driving them to commit that act. The act of intercourse was designed by GOD to create a union of mind, body, and spirit between two people. Having sex is not only a physical act but a spiritual one as well. When a person has sex with you they breathe into you a part of the spirit that is within them. Once the evil spirit of that predator enters men it leads them to believe that they will feel better or some of their pain will be relieved if they do to others what had been done to them. Once the evil spirit enters into women it acts like a comforter to soothe the pain and keep it pressed deep down in her psyche so that she can operate and function daily. The true mission of this spirit in women, however, is to keep them away from faithful men. The demon knows that if the woman ever forms a relationship with a faithful man its days of being able to reside in her are done.

Men, if you have ever been sexually abused or molested and have not cleansed yourself of the evil spirit associated with it, you must do it now. It is time to let it go. If you ever hope to become a faithful man, you must cleanse yourself. 1 John 3:3 says "And every man that has this hope in him purifies himself." Romans 12:1-2 exhorts us to submit our mind and body as a living sacrifice unto GOD. It is not telling us that this is something that GOD is going to do for us. Turning our mind and bodies away from sin and demonic influence is something that we have to do.

"Submit yourselves therefore to GOD. Resist the devil and he will flee from you. Draw near to GOD and HE will draw near to you. Cleans your hands… and purify your hearts… (James 4:7)."

Men, this applies to women too but mainly to you. In order to purify and cleans the evil spirit from your heart you have to resist doing anything that it normally leads you to do. You must essentially starve the devil to death. Once it is weak enough it will either die or flee from you to find another host. However, in order to move to another host it will lead you to molest or sexually abuse another person. If you want it to die within you, you will have to endure the war with it within yourself in order to overcome it and kill it. This will be a tough battle that may make you feel like you want to just die and get it over with but that is actually the demon crying out within you. You can beat it if you endeavor to endure, have a gut check, and just keep pressing your foot on its neck.

"Looking unto Jesus… who for the joy that was set before Him endured the cross, despising the shame… (and) consider Him that endured such contradiction of sinners (or evil spirits) against Himself lest you be weary and faint in your minds. You have not yet resisted unto blood, striving against sin (Hebrews 12:2-4)."

Men you have to resist unto the spilling of your own blood from within if necessary to kill the evil spirit that an evil person passed on to you. You must resist doing whatever it normally drives you to do with every fiber of your being until you choke it to death. Sometimes it won't be able to handle the pressure that you will place on it and it will flee on its own. During the process of resisting you can command it to leave. However, you must tell it where to go and command it never to return. The place where it must be commanded to go is back into hell. Be advised however that the last place an evil spirit wants to go is back into hell. This is why a whole legion of them that resided in one man were afraid of Jesus. They knew that He had the power to send them back to hell and they didn't want to go (Luke 8:27-33 and Mark 5:1-13). You have the power to cast the evil spirit out if you want it out. Just remember that losers focus on what they are going through but winners focus on what they are going to. Once you finish the fight you are going to be free of torment and captivity. So keep your eyes on the prize.

Now, women, this evil spirit that was transferred into you by a person who did something evil to you has to keep you out of the presence of faithful men. Therefore, it leads you to become attracted to some of the characteristics and qualities of the person who hurt you. This is the reason why you, and some of your girlfriends too, find yourselves with one abusive man after another. This evil spirit pretends to try to comfort you but its trick is to torment you. It leads you to keep the pain you feel pressed down deep inside of you but it also causes you to let it fly up in frightening fashion when a man does something to remind you of the one who hurt you. This is how that evil spirit plays to frighten faithful men away. It also knows that you need to release the pressure that you feel from its tormenting tricks periodically so it leads you to get that catharsis in the presence of other women. Its goal in that situation is to give you a feeling of being free but also to give it an opportunity to bring some of them into captivity.

The pressure that a woman feels from the torment of evil spirits begins to balloon on the inside. She reaches a point where she feels that she must either release her connection to the pain that is causing the pressure by either exploding or letting them go. However, the spirit that is tormenting her provides an alternative solution that will keep it in control "Just let it out, girl." Letting out is very much different than letting go. Letting something out does not mean breaking one's connection to it. It only allows one to let it out so that others can see it, but more importantly for the evil spirit, to be exposed to it.

Imagine, if you will, a woman with several balloons tied to her waist under her dress. The balloons represent the various issues in her life that is causing her mental and emotional pain. I have seen women let their issues float out while attending women's church conferences. The preacher or conference speaker leads the women with ties to emotional pain to open up and let those issues out. They are simply encouraged to let them out. Then the women are told that they must release them, however, no one actually teaches them how to release their pain or their connection to the evil spirit that is causing the pain. The predator that harmed you is no longer the source of the pain. They are long gone. The source of the pain is now the evil spirit that she continues to allow to live within her because it pretends to comfort her. It pretends to protect her from evil men when it actually prevents her from hooking up with a faithful man. She feels that she needs to remain connected to this spirit therefore she remains connected to her pain.

When a woman is led to let out her pain, imagine a

bunch of balloons coming out from under her dress and floating above her head. The preacher or speaker has gotten her to open up and expose her issues and to let other women see openly that she has been hiding pain deeply. But he does not seem to know how to get her to let them go. Why? Because it is not his job to lead her to let them go! GOD did not ordain him to do this, which is why the same women who go to a conference to get loosed one year have to go back next year to try and get loosed again.

The problem with opening herself up in a highly emotion charged atmosphere of a woman's conference is a woman can expose herself to the evil spirits floating around in there. Evil spirits thrives in atmospheres of intense emotional distress. It loves to hear people writhing and crying out of emotional pain. That reminds him of what it sounds like in hell where there is weeping and gnashing of teeth. The evil spirits can now identify which women in the conference are vulnerable to their attack. Since she opened herself up spiritually trying to release her issues or their associated pain that came from something other than sexual abuse or molestation, the evil spirits will try to enter her. She breathes the evil spirit in because the preacher or speaker inspires her to and its presence feels comforting. But a few days or weeks after attending the conference she will realize that she came home with more issues than she left with. I can tell you from personal experience that many of those women's conferences have hurt more women than they have helped. I have had to

Relationships

admit too many women to the hospital who became mentally disturbed from attending women's conferences or revivals. So, this is not something I heard about. I am sharing this with you from personal and professional experience.

Therefore, a woman must not open herself up and expose her issues without having help or knowing how to break the connection to them. I apologize to the liberated women for offending your feminine sensibilities. However, a woman cannot help another woman heal from emotional injury that was caused by a man. Ladies, when a woman comes to you who says she has a deliverance ministry it means that she needs to be delivered. She cannot do a thing for you, except make you feel good, but what she can do to you is breathe into you the evil spirit that she has tormenting her. The women who feel compelled to go out and minister to other women are being driven to do that by the evil spirit residing in them.

When women get together to discuss their painful experiences they think they are providing aid and comfort to one another. In fact, they are planting seeds of pain by exposing themselves to the spirits who torment that will bloom later. In their zeal to influence each other to "Let go and let GOD" (a phrase that has no practical meaning) they are actually allowing themselves to be exposed potentially to captivity. The words "influence" and "inspire" basically mean the same thing: to breathe into. The word influence is derived from the word "influenza". Influenza is obtained by being exposed to or allowing someone to breathe the virus that they have in them into you. When you allow yourself to be inspired or influenced by someone, whatever they have in them is going to be breathed into you. Inspiration and influence causes you to become "like" that person. Sometimes that is the goal we are trying to achieve but sometimes there is an unintended consequence that comes with it.

The remedy for emotional injury to a woman requires a man to fix the problem if a man caused the problem. That is the way GOD designed the system and there is nothing we can to do circumvent HIS system. This is what some people call "hair of the dog." If a problem was created by alcohol, it can be relieved by alcohol. The solution to most problems is in the thing that caused the problem. Curing a snake bite requires snake venom. If the problem was created through intimate contact, it must be resolved through intimate contact. Between men and women the intimate contact is physical: hand to hand, breast to breast, and mouth to mouth. Between men and men the intimate contact is hand to hand and head to head. A woman lets a man enter her heart and chase the evil spirit away. A man allows another man to enter that big ole cave in the heart of his mind to cast the evil spirit out. A woman may have gone to a psychiatrist or talked to a friend who helped her feel better. However, she was not cured. A man injured her so she needs a man who really truly loves her, a faithful man, to help her heal.

A man can help his wife eliminate the impact of her injury by touching, hugging, holding, and loving her at times other than when he is trying to lead her to sex. Constantly being tender with his wife will lead her to begin to lean on him for comfort rather than rely on the evil spirit. Then he has to lead her to combat the issues affecting her by teaching her how to confront them. Without confrontation there can be no resolution to any issue. She must confront them directly. Then she has to determine in her mind, from that moment on, those issues will no longer have an effect on her mind, body, soul, or spirit.

It is important that she forgive whoever she was hurt by, especially if it was by a close relative. She must conclude in her heart and mind that the problems they caused her is a result of a problem they have. It has nothing to do with her. In some cases the evil spirit torments their victim by making them believe they were somehow responsible for what happened to them. It also torments them by making them feel guilty for the pleasure their body may have experienced during the attack. This is the type of torment the evil spirit uses to cause the emotional and psychological distress to become very deep. Therefore, if a woman feels partly responsible for what others did to her, the best thing for her to do is to own it. Take the responsibility and then, along with the predator, she must determine to forgive herself. Just like the predator has forgiven himself, has moved on with his life, and is happy. She must also move on with her life and just be happy.

Women must understand that the purpose of the adversary sending his agents to rape a woman is to steal both her joy and virtue. He understands the power that is contained in a woman's virtue and he knows that her virtue is connected to her sexual purity. Therefore, he will send one of his disciples to molest a woman while she is a little girl, to rape her as a young woman, or to abuse her physically, mentally, and emotionally as an adult. The purpose of the attack, as many sociologists have discovered, has nothing to do with sex. It is about power and control. The agent of the adversary attacks women to control the power and virtue that women have in them and to prevent them from using that power to attack him. If they ever learned to break free of his torment and enter into a loving relationship with a faithful man, those two will be too powerful for him to deal with. They will be a threat to his very existence! Therefore, satan will do all that he can to attack a woman when she is the most vulnerable in order to keep her under his power and control. Not allowing oneself to forgive the devil's disciples for their deeds is in actuality giving him power and control over your destiny.

The enemy understands that he can bind, control, or prevent mankind from being free by influencing some men to oppress the powerful half of our population ourselves. He knows that men cannot produce children who are strong spiritually if their fathers oppress their mothers mentally, physically, and emotionally. The mothers cannot build up virtue or strength, power, and moral excellence in their children if those qualities were beaten out of her.

I understand that forgiving something that was and continues to be very painful is difficult. But if you command the mountain that is blocking the path to your destiny to be cast into the sea, and you believe it in your heart, it will be cast into the sea of forgiveness. Again, I know this is hard but you must get it done because not only is your financial and social status in jeopardy but your eternal life is also at risk.

When we hold the memory of hurt in our souls and fail to forgive those who caused it, as GOD instructed us to, it will say more about us on judgment day that it does the person whohurt us. If you don't forgive and learn to love, you can never live. You cannot grow into the person who GOD created you to be and you will never fulfill your destiny. If you never fulfill your destiny, you will never hear "Well done my good and faithful servant, enter into the joy of the Lord". Thus, you could lose your eternal life in heaven by holding on to the hurt you experienced on earth.

What the person did to you was wrong but the truth is GOD may or may not even punish them for it. You see, they may have already asked GOD for forgiveness, repented, forgiven themselves, and moved on with their life. They may not even remember you or what they did to you at this point in their lives. However, what is happening to you now, as a result of being unable to forgive and forget, you are in reality doing to yourself.

We seem to take morose pleasure or comfort in thinking about the person who hurt us. We fantasize about many tragedies befalling their lives. For some reason we think that they are constantly thinking about us when the reality is, 99 times out of 100, they are not. We could all stop caring so much about what people think about us if we knew how seldom they do. The person who harmed others don't want to remember or be reminded of the harm they caused. Therefore, they rarely if ever think about those who they harmed. We were once hurt by someone but now we are actually harming ourselves as we continue to hold on to the pain that they put us through and it causes us to suffer.

Pain is something that we experience which subsides after the stimulation that caused the pain ends or the injury has healed. Suffering is the result of pain that is held on to long after the stimulation that caused the pain is gone. Suffering comes as a result of failing to forgive. Suffering can last throughout eternity if we allow our identity to

Relationships

become synonymous with our injury. Once you die to the memory of that painful event the suffering will end. Then, you can grow to be that GOD created you to be, experience joyful relationships, fulfill your destiny, and prosper financially. Now, will you totally forget that it happened? No! But it just will not be in the forefront of your memory having an impact on what you can do or be.

You see, an apple seed must be willing to give up its life as a seed in order to become an apple tree. By contrast, we have to be willing to die to things that happened to us in the past in order to live and grow in love in the present. Each new day is a gift from GOD which is the reason why today is called "the present". Therefore, don't allow something that someone did to you in the past ruin your enjoyment of the love you could have in the present. Live today and forgive those who hurt you in the past so that you can enjoy the grace, peace, and beauty of love in the present.

Chapter 6
MEN vs. WOMEN

"If you want anything said, ask a man. If you want anything done, ask a woman." ~ Margaret Thatcher

The reason the average man does not understand women is because when GOD made Eve Adam was asleep. Men have very little insight into how the woman was built and have to either discover or be taught how a woman operates and why. Therefore, most of what women will want to do or desire to have in marriage will be illogical to their husbands. Men must remember that when GOD instructs us; tells us HIS wants, desires, or what HE wants us to do, it will be illogical as well. However, if we just do what GOD asks, we will achieve miraculous results. The same will be true if we just do what our wives ask us to do when they ask us to do it. Now, will most men just do what their wives ask? No. That is because too many men believe doing what their wife says many make them look henpecked. My brothers, there is nothing wrong with being henpecked if you are pecked by a good hen.

Men can receive miraculous results in their marriage if they learn to give in more often to their wives. In every case where it does not make a difference or take the family off course in terms of finances or achieving your goals, the husband should let his wife have her way. In every case where it does not make a difference, he should let her do things her way. GOD has given men good physical strength and he gave women great spiritual power. When a man gives in to his wife's desires it will cause her to move into proper position with her husband and will give him an opportunity to access her power.

We live in two dimensions simultaneously: the physical and spiritual. That is, where we live and where GOD resides respectively. Everything that exists in the physical originated in the spiritual. Women have a greater ability to access the creative power of the spiritual realm than men. A woman that is in proper position with her husband has the power to see what GOD sees. When GOD has a vision planned for a family, HE will tell the man about the vision but HE will show the vision to the man's wife. When he comes to explain to his wife what GOD told him about that vision, she will say "I can see it!" The godly vision for a family is more likely to be fulfilled whenever the wife is in proper position with her husband. The power to receive the vision rests within him. The spiritual and creative power to make it manifest actually resides in her. Women are life givers. They give birth to everything in the earth. GOD designed the woman in a way that empowers her with the ability to give birth to whatever she is able to see. If she can see it as it exists in the spiritual dimension, she will be able to deliver or birth it into the physical dimension.

A good wife is a mirror to her husband. Whatever is in him or whatever she thinks about him, he should be able to see in her eyes. If he is endeavoring to do or become something and she can see it in him, she can help him give birth to it. Now men can have difficulty in accepting help from women because the help women want to give seems illogical to them. Since a woman is a man's mirror, whatever she does will appear to be backward to him. Men will often reject the woman's help because what she wants to do appears to be 180 degrees out of phase with what he is trying to do.

When a couple is dancing, a Waltz for example, the woman is following the man's lead and doing the same thing he is doing but it will be backwards or a mirror reflection of what he is doing. When a wife does or suggests something to help her husband achieve the family's vision, she will be following her husband's lead but to him it will appear to be backward. So a husband has to recognize that his wife is a mirror. If she shows him something, it will appear to be backward. But, if he listens to her, although it appears to be backward, it will help move him forward.

One of the main differences between men and women that produce conflict is in how they were created. Men were created out of dirt but the woman was built from bone that came from the inside of a man (Genesis 2:7 & 21). Consequently, men have a tendency to gravitate toward the dirt. This is why men are bottom line oriented in problem solving, want to get to the heart of a matter, or uncover the root cause. A man has an inherent desire to get to the bottom line quickly or to get back to the dirt.

A woman's inherent nature in resolving conflict in her marriage is to get to the root or bottom line by trying to get inside of her husband. She will always try to find the answer to whatever the problem or conflict is in their family inside of him. This is why she will always try to find out what he is thinking or how he is feeling. Her effort to root around on the inside of her man feels like an irritating poking or prodding to him. It becomes painful sometimes to men when their wife constantly pokes because she starts to feel like a thorn in their side. However, men must understand that when the woman does this she has spotted, sensed, or is trying to prevent some sort of trouble. Therefore, she is trying to get to the root or her bottom line which is in his bone or under his skin.

Since Eve was built with a rib bone from her husband's side (under his skin) the heart of the matter or root cause of any issue in a woman's family, from her perspective, is inside or under the skin of her husband. If it feels like she is getting under your skin men. If she pokes, pushes, and prods you to open up to her brothers, you have to let her in. She is trying to get in when she wants to know how you feel or asks "what cha thinkn".

This question drives most men crazy but a man has to allow his wife to do what she is naturally designed to do which is to get inside of you. GOD made her to be bone of your bone and flesh of your flesh. She will continue to get under your skin and make you mad to the bone until you allow her to live, move, and have her being inside of you. Brothers, if you don't let her do what she needs to do you are going to have a problem. So, in order for you to have harmony and peace in your home, you will have to let her inside of you!

Now once you let her inside be prepared for her to redecorate the place. Once a man gets married on the outside, most of us keep our secret bachelor pad on the inside. To understand what happens next, men, you have to have seen a woman in action when she enters a single man's house. The first thing she does is look around to see what changes need to be made. Our favorite musty old couch that we spent many hours sleeping on, and have broken in just right, is the first thing that she will want to throw out. To a woman the bed is for sleeping in.

She will want to do the same thing with her man's physical house. The simple bachelor apartment that we retained inside of our minds after we got married will be transformed into a split level home filled with flowers, plants, and potpourri. A man may own a house but the wife will transform the house into a home. She will also transform her single minded man into a husband.

Relationships

Men, we must submit to this change and let our wives inside to help transform us from the beer drinking frat boy that we used to be into the mature minded man that she needs us to be. This transformation will equip us to guide, guard, and govern; direct, correct, and protect a family properly.

Good leaders are created by those they are leading. One of the keys to successful leadership is in allowing those who are being led to have input into how they are led. A husband will become a successful leader for his wife when he allows her to give advice and guidance to her leader. In describing how GOD would transform the bride of Christ, Jesus said that HE would give her "beauty for ashes". When a man allows his wife to help transform him internally, from single frat boy to a married man, she will give him beauty for ashes. The next time she puts lotion on your hands or arm externally, brothers, you will know that she wants to do the same thing internally; to give you beauty for ashy.

Now, men, women are also more affected by and attracted to nature than we are which is why they love flowers and we could care less. Nature has a direct impact on a woman's being as a girl becomes a woman with her 1st menstruation. Nature does this to her. A new moon appears in the sky every 28 days and every 28 days a woman begins a new menstruation cycle. Have you ever wondered why people seem to go crazy when there is a full moon? I am not going to answer that question because I'm not crazy!

Anywaaaaay... A woman is a vehicle of life, giving life and nourishment in a manner identical to mother earth. A boy does not have a dramatic impact of nature to mark his movement into manhood. The average boy has to be turned into a man and literally trained, if not forced, to become a servant of something greater than himself. Women seem to naturally grow into this responsibility. Thus, they appear to be more spiritually oriented and seem to naturally know how to care for a baby. A boy, on the other hand, needs a man to lead him through this process. However, he needs a mother to teach him how to love and feel empathy for others.

A man and woman must be involved in the life and development of a child and a boy in particular. This is critical because a woman is the vehicle of nature whereas a man is the force of life in a civilized society. A mother is the teacher and guide for a child who nurtures, shapes and molds them into the person they were created to be. A mommy moderates a child's natural character from selfishness, war, and conflict to selflessness, peace and love. A father is the governor of a child's civil order and social purpose and has the duty to lead a child into his or her destiny. Mommy prepares the person or determines who the child will be. Daddy determines destiny. How he leads will have a great impact on what a child will do.

Now, many men in today's society have a problem leading because they have never been affirmed and confirmed by a father. GOD trained, developed and confirmed leadership in Adam before HE gave him Eve. Today, most men are forced to develop into leaders on their own after they receive a wife. The problem with this is woman has some intuitive idea of what her husband should be doing. Therefore, she can see when her husband is winging it or just trying to fake it until he can make it. She knows that he is not doing what she believes he should be doing. Yet, he tries to cover his lack of knowledge by pretending that he knows until he learns but she already knows that he doesn't know.

The problem the average man has in this situation is he knows that he doesn't know, but he doesn't want anyone to know that he doesn't know. He will get offended if his wife questions whether he knows what he is doing. Then, they will fight and argue (Be a man!). Although they love each other, their marriage can very well be destroyed due to his lack of knowledge. He will appear to her to be immature and will begin to look for a man who will be a man. Thus a man who is married must get the knowledge he needs to remain married. A lot of this knowledge can come from his wife.

TAKING RESPONSIBILITY AND POWER IN RELATIONSHIPS

I was giving a seminar one day "Finding Your Personal Fortune" and I asked the question: "Do you know why the average young adult is living in poverty?" The answer was going to be as a result of having too many babies without being married. A young woman about 25 years old chimes in and said: "It could be that the woman had sorry a$$ men in her life or because she only has enough to take care of her three kids."

The purpose of the seminar was to show how good relationships are the foundation of every good fortune. But her answer took "The Relationship Doctor" right into the heart of that problem as she stated it. I contend that if we always focus on what the other person in the relationship is doing or have done we will never see how what we were doing or had done contributed to the problem. We will always remain in a cycle of poverty if we cannot see and accept our part of the responsibility for what that relationship turned out to be. We will just continue to make the same mistakes over and over. Therefore, as a means of getting the audience's attention (because I knew the atmosphere was about to get intense), I asked her a barrage of questions:

At what point does a young woman with three kids stop blaming men and start taking responsibility for their actions? After she has had ONE sorry man why is it that she couldn't recognize sorry when she met the other two men? After she had been left with a baby by one sorry

Relationships

man why did she have babies for another TWO sorry men? If the babies are by the same sorry man, how can a woman continue to have baby after baby for a man who is sorry? Is it just the man who is sorry?

Women have a huge amount of social, political, financial and sexual power. It is time for young women to start utilizing their power and stop playing the victim. Just because a woman was once a victim it does not mean that she must continue to allow herself to be victimized. Women have power because they represent over 53% of the population in America. Women also represent 50% of the work force in America. I apologize in advance for being crass but that means women control half the money and all of the pu$$y in America. The two things that men spend most of their waking hours chasing is money and pu$$y.

Women have to start using the Power of the P and stop giving it to men who are sorry. Women have to start utilizing the power of the Purse and stop allowing men to live with them who are sorry. It is easy to recognize a man who is sorry. Most of the time that man is an unashamed NINJA (No Income No Job or Assets). If her man is a NINJA a woman can't complain if he goes out dressed in black at night sneaking around trying to find women to cheat on her with.

The TRUE purpose for sex is not just pleasure but for

making babies. A young woman can't lie down and commit an act that can make babies with a man who can't take care of himself. If he can't take care of himself, how is he going to take care of her and her babies? C'mon ladies! Is it the man who is sorry or is it that women are setting the conditions for men to BE sorry? Only a woman can breed a dog. A dog can want to bury his bone but only a woman can give him a place to bury it. If women stop participating in dog-like behavior with men, men will have no choice but to stop being dogs. If women stop allowing men to be sorry; if they demanded that a man work every day before he can come to her to get a lay, perhaps they wouldn't be as sorry as they are today! Women have the power to make men be men. Women have to begin to start utilizing that power.

The following is a tag line from a Coty Perfume commercial: "Want him to be more of a man? Try being more of a woman!" We are living in a paradox wherein GOD designed the man to lead but they don't lead because women don't establish a standard of conduct that demands that they lead. Now, it is a tough paradox for women to deal with, sort of like the chicken or the egg question, because men won't lead unless women take the lead and demand that they lead. On the other hand, men won't do what they are supposed to do because women don't do what they must do. However, it is critical to the future of their children that women demand that a man be a man in order to be with them sexually and have babies. Women need strong productive men to have babies with because a chump can't raise a champ.

MEN VS WOMEN IN DATING

Too many women make the mistake of thinking a man just wants to have a woman with a nice ass at home when most men really want that ass to also be an asset. Women don't want a man they have to take care of and neither do men. Men also want a woman who can immediately bring something, like a positive cash flow, to the table. For some reason there are a lot of women who believe that because they have a pretty face, a big butt, and big boobs, a man is supposed to open up his bank account to them. Like Jamie Foxx says "If all you got is love (re: sex), I don't need it"! When a real man is ready to marry he will not want an economic NINJA (No Income No Job or Assets) sneaking around trying to figure out how to get access to his bank account. He will want a woman that can be a worker, wife, mother, homemaker, and lover. She must know how to make dough AND bake it.

This is especially true if she is a professional woman and wants a man who is professional too. He will respect her career but he will also expect her to handle her duties at home. This may be too much for women who are looking for a man to make life easy for them. But here is the GOD given truth ladies: In the beginning (Genesis 2:20) GOD created the woman to be a "help meet" that is a suitable, proper, and fit helper for a man. 1 Corinthians 11:9 says "Neither was the man created for the woman but the woman for the man." You see, a woman does not really need help but a man does! So GOD created her to help him!

You hear women say all the time "I don't really need a man for anything." Frankly, for the most part, that is true. However, GOD knew that a man would need a woman so HE made the woman to give a man the suitable, proper and fitting help that he would need. Yet, women today try to flip the script and make the male/female relationship about helping them. The woman wants to inspect a man to see what he has to offer her. In reality, she must actually inspect him to discover where she can help or find out what she can do for him. If she helps direct him into the fullness of his better self, then all that she needs financially will come to her but through him. GOD gave a woman power to help deliver a man into wealth. Therefore, ladies, it is not what a man can do for you. The key is you and what you can do for a man! In order to find the right man for you, you have to be the right woman for that man. Now, ladies, it is not wise to condition a man to discover his better self and prepare him to produce wealth if you are not married to him. He can easily walk away from you with a total makeover and go to another woman who will reap the benefits of your work. Therefore, make sure you are married to a man who you help to make wealthy. If he decides to leave, you can be compensated in the divorce settlement.

True love will prevent divorce but it requires a real sacrifice. A sacrifice wherein we are willing to lose our life as we have known it in order to have a new life in love. When we express our love with flowers, the flower has to be willing to sacrifice its life to allow us to express our love. When the recipient of the flower loves or has an appreciation for the sacrifice the flower made, he or she will try to keep it alive for as long as possible by placing it in water, caring for it, and sharing part of his or her life by giving it attention.

By contrast a woman for a man is like a rose. She gives him something soft, delicate, and sweet to love, care for, and help to grow or appreciate. Anything that someone appreciates they will help it to grow. To appreciate in this context means to increase in value. Women have to make the sacrifice of cutting away the stem that nourished them, the thorns that protected them, and the roots that connected them to the elements that gave birth to them. A woman must then allow herself to rest in her husband's hands to receive nourishment through him, to be protected by him, and to be reconnected to her roots through his so that their children can have common roots. Men who love and care for their wives will have an appreciation for the sacrifice she made. Men who love and appreciate their wives have heart to give her something that she likes, wants or needs to help her grow or increase in value. Being of greater value to and within herself will allow her to also be of greater value to and for her husband. Real appreciation causes a cycle of love, sharing and caring to rebound to itself over and over again.

Through love, sacrifice and appreciation a woman has the power to help make a man wealthy. Women need to recognize and men need to learn how to utilize this power. After GOD created the woman for the man HE made this statement in Deuteronomy 8:18 "But thou shalt remember the Lord thy GOD for it is HE that giveth thee power to get wealth..." The power that GOD gave man to get wealth is the woman. Examine the people you know who are wealthy to see if this is true. "Whoso findeth a wife findeth a good, and obtains favor of the Lord (Proverbs 18:22)."The men who partner with a "good" wife (one who is like merchandise or something of value) always seem to proper. Those who partner with a woman who doesn't recognize her "good" or value usually end up in divorce. So, ladies, find the man who your good (that is, your gifts, talents, and abilities) fit best. Get married and then get ready for a fast exciting ride to success.

Most married men don't become wealthy because they have not learned to recognize and utilize their wives' good or value. GOD created a man to lead and take authority. Yet, I don't see very many men who have learned how to lead or who have already paid the cost to be the boss. Too

Relationships

many of them want a woman to just give them the lead and allow them take authority when they have not demonstrated that they are worthy of being followed. But women do give them the lead and when they jack everything up the woman trys to take the lead herself and the problems begin. Women must set a standard for men otherwise we will have these debates, gender duels, and discussions perpetually.

A lack of proper leadership or knowledge on how to lead a woman often leads to an attempt to dominate. The only men who feel they need to dominate a woman are those who lack knowledge. They feel they must force a woman to submit to their will physically because they do not have the knowledge to lead her to follow their will intellectually. The best leaders are able to motivate a woman to follow their will because they want to not because they have to. Men must learn that they have to pay the cost to be the boss. Some of that cost involves listening to and following the advice of their wife. The best things in life, including the best women, are placed on a high shelf. The only way that a man will be able to reach that high is by the books that he stands on. The more books he reads on how to lead a wife and family the higher he will be able to reach.

When a man really loves a woman he must provide her with three things, which are the essential elements of love: freedom, justice, and equality. Notice there is no dominion involved in any of them. When GOD gave dominion over the earth to man (that is the species, not the gender, which includes women), the list of things man was given dominion over did not include people (Genesis 1:28). A man has to learn to lead people yet have dominion over his environment. He cannot think that he can have dominion over his wife and family. If he does not learn how to lead and guide them gently, he will lose them eventually.

A woman is like a rose. She has petals that are beautiful, delicate, soft, and smells so sweet. But a rose also has a thick stem with thorns. The thick stem represents the toughness she must have in order to stand in the midst of all the problems and challenges the world forces her to face. The thorns have grown on her tough exterior as a defense mechanism to protect and to painfully "prick" those men who try to touch her that do not know how to properly handle her.

A man was designed by GOD to be a husbandman to the rose. He must care for, nurture, and protect her so that she can flourish, achieve maximum potential, and radiate beauty. The stem is used by the rose to access the water and nourishment she needs from the dirt. She gets the light she needs from the sun. A man must care for and lead a woman in a way that causes her to allow him to clip away her stem and lay gently in his hands. A man was created by GOD from water and dirt so his woman should be able to get all the nourishment she needs through him. Then he must lift her up to the light of the Son. In return, she should empower him or make him look and/or be better through her softness, grace, beauty, and sweetness. Through this practice of leading and loving properly and the combination of her qualities a woman will be able to transform a man's heart.

When you think of a man's heart, ladies, you have to think of it in 4 but mainly 3 contexts: the heart of the man, the heart of the mind, and the heart of the matter. The 4th context is his physical heart or blood pump which is never really an issue or topic of discussion unless he is having trouble with it.

The heart of the matter is something men are powerfully oriented toward. We want to get to the heart or bottom of things quickly. Not to be crass but this is the reason why a man always tries to get a woman to have sex with him soon after meeting him. He is oriented toward getting to her bottom. Therefore, a woman, unless she is just trying to get him, cannot let him. This can damage a woman mentally and emotionally but it has an impact on the man spiritually (Proverbs 7:1-23). The heart of the man is his "spirit", the real him, his inner nature or inner being. This is the source from which his character and qualities are derived.

The heart of the mind is a man's process center; the place where he makes all of his decisions and the place where he both discovers and stores his feelings. If you ever ask a man what he thinks about a particular subject, he will often preface his response with "I feel…" A man's feelings begin in his mind. If a woman suddenly asks a man "Do you love me?" he has to think about it for a minute... or two... or three. The way that a man feels about a woman is strongly correlated with how he thinks about her. They say that the way to a man's heart is through is stomach. "They" are wrong about this one also. The way to a man's heart is actually through his mind. If a woman wants a man to get into her, she has to get into his head. She has to make him begin to think about her.

A lot of single people are looking to be married but too many have very little knowledge about how to be and remain married.They have little or no clue as to the sacrifices they will have to make in order to make the marriage work. The symbol of love and marriage is the valentine. The two sides of a valentine actually represent life and death. Each time the heart beats or pumps blood out it stops for a fraction of a second. In order to be in love with someone or to become married a person must die to their single life. A bride and groom wear black and white to symbolize death and life respectively. A couple who gets married must willingly die to their single lives in order to be resurrected into new life as one if they intend to be married. To be IN love, we must die to ourselves, become selfless and egoless, and dedicate our life to providing aid and comfort to the one we love. Those who struggle in life, love and marriage are those who refuse to die to their former selves.

Another thing "they" are wrong about is "A woman has to kiss a lot of frogs in order to find a prince." A lot of women are kissing frogs and getting hurt in the process. Here's a Muppet News flash: Kissing frogs will only turn you into a frog. A person will ultimately become what they kiss. The wholesale leaping from frog to frog or man to man will end once women get the type of knowledge that leads to wisdom rather than operating on knowledge that comes from experience. "They" say that experience is the best teacher. However, "they" are wrong again! Wisdom is actually the best teacher. Wisdom will teach a young woman not to give her body to a man who is not her husband. Experience will only teach her that she shouldn't have done it! Pain comes with experience whereas wisdom helps a woman avoid painful experiences.

We will never live long enough to make all of the mistakes there are in the world to learn all of the knowledge we need from bad experiences and we certainly can't afford to pay for them all. As a result of following conventional wisdom, bad relationship advice, or what "they" say many women are going through painful experiences with a number of men over and over again. Like the frogs they have been kissing, women jump from one man to another carrying the baggage that she packed from dealing with the previous men. Carrying baggage, ladies, is like walking out of the restroom with the hem of your dress stuck in the back of your underwear. You think you have yourself covered but everyone can see your back side.

In today's economy, if you want to travel with extra baggage, you have to pay for it. If you have a problem socializing at work because of something that happened to you as a child, it will eventually become reflected in your resume and cost you to lose opportunities for raises and promotions.

In today's society, if you want to carry baggage from previous relationships into the next relationship you will have to pay in terms of missing the opportunity to make the ultimate merger. It doesn't take long for someone who is interested in, and examining, you to see that something is wrong when you are carrying baggage. You may think you have it covered but it doesn't stay hidden long. Eventually, something that Ray does will remind you of Jamal and you will show your @$$.

When I decided to get married, I got rid of all of the gifts other women had given me. Clothing, jewelry, watches, shoes, paintings, plants, etc; everything was gone. I did not want to bring anything that I had picked up from other women into my marriage. The bad taste and residual ache from disappointments, betrayals, broken heartedness, etc all had to go too. They had to be dropped at the curb like leaving luggage with a Sky Cap. The only difference is I had to send that baggage to a place where I never intend to travel.

Before we move into a new home, we separate everything that we don't intend to take with us from the old home. Once we decide to enter a new relationship or climb to a new level, whether it be personally or professionally, it will be difficult to do carrying excess baggage. We must determine then to leave some old bags behind or unpack (intentionally forget) some of the things we had been traveling with in order to successfully reach and remain on the new level.

The thing a MAN (man sized boys are different) needs from a woman is not just understanding and support but also a challenge and a push to be the best we can be as men, in our aspirations and usual vocations. Women seem to naturally do this for their man and their children. Yet, their girlfriends just get support. I've noticed women don't like to tell their girlfriends the truth when they think it will hurt her feelings. Consequently women don't often get good relationship advice from each other. Much like Janet did in the movie "Why Did I Get Married", ladies please give your girlfriends the advice they need to avoid the bad and learn how to get it right with the good men.

I am using broad strokes to paint the picture of men and women because I must speak generally or highlight the issues that affect everyone generally. It is my hope that you will take the issues as presented generally and use them to develop a plan to improve your relationships individually. A man is doomed to failure in a relationship if he tries to figure out all women's minds and treat them as if they are one. Women are much too varied individually and complicated intellectually and emotionally. The reciprocal is true for men. Women cannot place all men in a box. However, it is critically necessary that men and women figure out their spouse's mind to make sure their thinking is on one accord. A married couple who constantly sees things different ways, have different solutions for solving problems or achieving goals are on a divided course and will end up in divorce.

Finally, most of the trouble enters the relationship during the mate selection process. When a person meets or first begins dating they are on their best behavior. During the initial dates most people present themselves as if they are the 1 when they are actually a 0 who knows how to pretend to be the 1. We get excited because we think that we have found the 1. But this is the time for pulling back and putting on our thinking cap.

In our system of integers we tend to count: 1-2-3, etc, and we teach our children to count like that initially. This practice causes us to forget that the 0 actually comes first. Dating is a numbers game. The more people who we encounter the more likely we are to find or discover

Relationships

the 1 that is right for us. Every numbers game follows the rules of mathematics. The rules of mathematics never change. Therefore, when we are looking for the 1 a 0 is always going to show up first. The problem with the 0 is he/she knows how to look like the 1. They present themselves as having value when they have no value at all. Ultimately, when the 1 does show up, who will actually be good for us, we are often stuck with the 0 that doesn't know how to even be good.

To make matters worse, we also forget that there are negative numbers in our system of integers. A person can be a 1 but he or she is actually a negative 1. So we get rid of that person and find another 1 only to discover that they are negative 2. Therefore, we must have some knowledge, a plan, a system that we can use to differentiate the 0s from the 1s and the positives from the negatives.

The product of good love is multiplication (be fruitful and multiply). What we should get from the proper application of love is a good product. The correct answer to a multiplication problem is the right product. So, you see GOD knew exactly what HE was doing. We can never get a positive product when we try to multiply with either a negative or a zero.

WOMEN VS WOMEN

It is becoming increasingly clear that women are

going to have to leave the echo chamber of their circle of girlfriends and begin to actually talk to men about dating and relationships. Women may actually learn more and perhaps get the information they really need to get the type of man they really want if they begin to listen to men rather than their girlfriends.

Many women don't have a man or have difficulty with their men because they make relationship decisions based on the experiences or advice of their friends. This can be expensive in terms of the amount of time spent with the wrong man and the amount of pain that they had to endure. The least expensive method of learning to understand and finding the right man is finding those men that have wisdom, who can teach you what to do as well as what not to do, and then follow their guidance. Nobody knows men and what they do to use and abuse women better than men. Men know how to identify a woman who is a "keeper" and would best be able to explain to a woman what a man would be looking for.

Often the WORST advice a woman can get about relationships and men is from other women. Again, ladies, you have to begin to listen to men (fathers, brothers, uncles, cousins, friends, etc) who care for you about how to deal with men. Your girlfriends are not getting it right but they are the ones who you listen to and go to for advice.

Women don't want to tell their girlfriends (although

Relationships

they really love them) the truth when it comes to relationships because they don't want to hurt her feelings. A surgeon has to cut a patient and leave them in temporary pain in order to relieve or save them from long term pain. If the person does not get the operation they will live with more pain. You see, trying to support someone who is in pain by not telling them the truth leads to more pain. If your girlfriend was holding her hand down on a hot stove and telling you that it hurts, what would you say? "Awww girl, it will be ok. It will hurt for awhile but you will get through it." NO, you will tell her to take her hand off the damn heat! And you know you wouldn't be nice too about it either. You would say, "Damn, girl, just lift up your hand! GOD, that is so dumb." So why do women react differently when their girlfriends are being hurt by men?

Ladies from now on you must begin to tell your girlfriends the truth. It might be painful to hear but it will save her the pain of heartache in the long run. Plus you may save her a lot of time being with a loser that will only end up leaving her with some type of STD or HPV. When your girlfriend is going through some stupid trouble with some dumb dude deep down inside you know exactly what your girl needs to do. If you really love her, you can't be afraid to tell her the truth! Don't just try to encourage her to be strong and to hold on. Tell her the truth.

From a man's perspective I would have to say to her "Yes, you are strong but why must you deliberately put yourself through tests of strength? Why do you allow yourself to struggle through or try to make it through things that you don't have too? Don't you believe there is a man or men out there who will care for, love, and respect you without making you have to "go through" drama or heart trauma? WHY must you torture yourself when you don't have too? You are choosing to go through this and you know you have been here with this joker before. So you have to ask yourself WHY. WHY don't you feel that you deserve to be happy? WHY must you continually pick men and choose to remain with men who make you unhappy? WHY?"

You see, most of the women giving relationship advice (with a few exceptions) aren't getting it and haven't gotten it right yet. Many women who like to give other women relationship advice are still suffering the effects of painful relationships themselves. These women think that because they have been through a lot of crap with men, they will be able to help other women build healthy relationships with men. Giving advice to another person, ministering from a position of pain, is a terrible thing to do to a person because it only leads to more pain. The only people who you can take advice from concerning relationships are those who are single. That is those who are whole within themselves and connected and one with GOD. Don't make the mistake of confusing a person who goes to church and quotes scripture with one who is single. Sometimes they are the ones who are the most damaged or

Relationships

still carrying residual damage and are in denial about it. Many people who give advice, although they reference GOD, are not yet connected and one with GOD. It may sound good but you will know when it is not GOD when their advice does not match up with the word of GOD. They may be sincere but they will be sincerely wrong.

Many people can quote the bible and know what the bible says but there are very few who know how to use it and make it benefit their lives. I have seen women who were being horribly abused by their husband being advised by church going bible quoting women to stay in the marriage and just submit to their husband. They try to make the woman feel guilty about wanting to leave by telling them that GOD hates divorce. However, GOD also said that a man should love his wife as he loves himself. If the man is not kicking his own @$$ periodically, then he does not love his wife and she should leave.

There are church going bible quoting women who advise other women to wait for GOD to send them a husband. GOD will send a woman a husband but the way that knowledge is applied has to be placed in proper context. If you try to follow it as presented, it will lead you into yet another relationship wreck. First of all, GOD will not send a woman a man that is GOOD for her until she is good for him. She must be ready (prepared herself and is single) to receive a good man. GOD is not going to send a woman a good man when she still has the spirit of bad men living within and tormenting her. Tyler Perry said "It is hard to love a good woman after she has had a bad man." Sending a good man who has prepared himself to receive a good woman to a woman who is still broken and in pain is not fair to that good man.GOD would not do that. A good man may see her need and decide to take on the responsibility to try to fix it. However, GOD would not do that to him unless HE first showed the man what he would be getting into and allowed him to make a choice.

Many church going women are often still in pain but also in denial about it. Because they go to church regularly they try to assume that GOD has made them whole. Here is a quite secret (in my low whispering voice). GOD is not going to heal you from that pain. You have to do it yourself (Romans 12:1-2, 1 John 3:3, Ephesians 5:26-27). You have to take yourself through a purification process to purge yourself of the spirits of men. This process may take 3-5 years and it requires abstaining from sex. Letting more men in, while trying to clear the old men out, just makes a bigger mess. If a woman wants GOD to send them a good man, they must become complete in themselves or complete and HIM. If they don't do what they need to do, GOD is not going to do what they want HIM to do. GOD will not set a good man up for that kind of trouble? GOD would not double cross a good man who has been trying to live right like that! So here is what actually happens ladies when you are waiting for GOD to send you a man:

Relationships

The devil is ALWAYS going to send a man who is not good first!

As I said previously, trying to find the right mate is a numbers game. When we are looking for the 1 a 0 is always going to show up first. GOD will allow this to happen because HE will want to see if you know enough or are spiritually discerning enough to be able to tell the 1 from the 0. Women often fail in selecting the right mate, especially when they are waiting on GOD to send them a good man, because they do not realize that the 0 is always going to show up before the 1.

Now because the 0 naturally comes first, he knows how to come to you looking like he is the 1. The enemy has been watching what you watch so he knows what you are attracted to. He listens to what you tell your girlfriends about the man who makes you hot in the pants. Then he sends you one of his disciples who is that type of man. Never forget now that this guy will always show up before the one who is really right for you. The devil will give you the type of man you want but GOD cannot give you the type of man you need until you have prepared yourself and are ready to receive him.

Living life is like playing a game of checkers with GOD. GOD has a move and we have a move. Because GOD is faithful, just, and won't cheat, HE is NOT going to move out of turn. When it is our turn to move GOD is going to just wait until WE make OUR move before HE takes HIS next move. However, we will cry and say "I need you to come now, Lord, and do something!" However, GOD will say "No, it's your move baby girl". The point is, we have a move and GOD has a move. GOD is never going to move out of turn. Once GOD has made HIS move it is up to us now to make our move. Therefore, we have to do what we can do so that GOD can do what HE can do.

On the seventh day GOD rested. That means that GOD as ALREADY done everything that HE is going to do to provide for you including making the person already who is good and right for you. When you are ready to receive that person you will find them right in front of you. You won't have to look for them or pray for them. When you are ready he/she will appear. There is an old saying "When the student is ready, the teacher will appear." Well, the same is true for relationships. When a virtuous woman is ready, the faithful man will appear and vice versa. The key, ladies, is to stop listening to bad advice from other women and do what you have to do to prepare yourself to receive the right man.

Finally, women have to stop encouraging each other to jump into sexual relationships with men. For some reason too many women believe that having sex with a man reserves for them a special place in his life with special privileges. It does not. Most men will take the free sex but they are not going to place a high value on a woman

Relationships

who gives herself away easily. In the black community that is called "acting hoochie". In my mom's day, when a woman was acting hoochie other women would check her. If the women were all in the kitchen, for example, and one woman was in the living room with the men, the other women would go get her. Women can help lead each other to have better relationships with men by encouraging each other to holdout until after they have passed the altar. All the sex in the city type sleeping around has not worked to women's advantage. It has left many women stuck raising children alone. Women must encourage each other stop the real life sex in the city activity.

BLACK WOMEN VS WHITE WOMEN

There is a war going on between black women and white women over rich black men of which the average white woman may not be aware. White women don't seem to be obsessed with the subject as black women appear to be. White women are simply going about the business of being themselves. If they find a man that they like and he happens to be black, they govern themselves accordingly to get his attention and make the acquisition. The acquisition for them more often than not leads to marriage. Black women are baffled as to why black men, especially the rich ones, can seem to just leave them behind and run off with the white woman so easily. Therefore, black women create myths about white women that serve to explain why the black man chooses the white woman. Sometimes black women choose to place a label on white women such as "gold digger" to suggest that they were only after the black man's money.

The gold digger label may properly characterize some. However, I contend that gold diggers satisfy a need and should be compensated accordingly. I know that sounds crazy but here's what I mean. Gold diggers are usually young attractive women who are attracted to wealthy men. Most wealthy men need to be attractive to and receive the attention of young attractive women. Gold diggers like to give attention to and receive compensation from wealthy men. These men like gold diggers and the gold diggers like them. Therefore, neither of them complain about the other because they both get what they want.

The only women who complain and label other women gold diggers are those women who are jealous. The only men who complain are those men that are material rich and cash poor. They present the image of being rich because they have cars, clothes, and jewelry but they have no cash. These men don't understand that whatever you can put on your ass is not an asset. A woman will get with this man thinking she will be able to live comfortably, not to get what he's got. But once she discovers he has been playing "fake it till you make it" she will take off and try to take as much compensation as she can with her. He will call her a gold digger by claiming she just wanted his money to cover up the fact that he tried to deceive her.

For some reason professional class black women do not appear to be as upset about the blue collar black men who marry white women. They don't see the white women who are with a regular everyday working guy as gold diggers because the average guy in that status does not have any gold. What they don't realize however is some guys like this are rich but not wealthy. Gold diggers are attracted to wealthy men, not rich men. There is a difference. The thing that white women seem to realize that black women totally miss is the right woman can make the right man rich. Those riches can then be made into wealth.

Rather than helping to make a man rich and then helping to lead him into wealth, black women, particularly the professional class, want black men to already have riches or wealth in order to be with them. The main problem that black women have in this regard is they often don't have access to wealthy black men. Wealthy black men usually have a white business manager, lawyer, agent, accountant, etc., who is going to invite them to parties where only white women or black women married to white men are invited. They will continuously get exposed to white woman after white woman until they eventually pick one. These women won't necessarily be rich or wealthy therefore black women will tend to label them gold diggers because it looks to them like they are going for the brother's gold. However, the men don't care that the women don't have any money. What they intend to bank on is how the woman's perceived virtue can increase their value or improve their economic position in their company or social circle.

Most black men would rather have a black woman. However they want a real black woman who understands the value of her virtue, is confident with her own brand of beauty, one who is not caught up in the feminist movement, and one who knows how to be a partner with her husband rather than a competitor.Black men want a woman who understands how to nurture her man; to help him bring out his better nature so that he can be his best self personally and professionally. The more a wife can help a man better himself the better he can be for his wife. This is what most rich, wealthy or professional class black men want but what they get from too many black women is: "Be a man! Why I got ta nurture yo big dumb @$$."

Rather than women classifying white women who they perceive to be going after the brother's money as gold diggers black women should actually try to learn what white women are doing to capture the hearts of wealthy black men. As the old saying goes "If you can't beat'em join'em." White women are often able to swim with the sharks or the whales because they learn how to be Pilot fish. Sharks and whales usually have Pilot fish with them because they like following them. Pilot fish like getting

Relationships

fed and receiving protection. The sharks and whales don't mind the Pilot fish being there because they provide a benefit that helps keep the sharks and whales healthy.

Chapter 7
BOYS SHOULD PLAY WITH DOLLS

"Men do not quit playing because they grow old, they grow old because they quit playing." ~ Oliver Wendell Holmes

Women in our society appear to be more responsible than men in the areas of marriage and family. Women seem to naturally know how to take responsibility for being a wife, mother, and home maker whereas men seem to have to grow into the responsibilities of husband, father and in some cases provider. As I thought about how this difference came to be, I realized that it is rooted in how little girls play compared to little boys.

A little girl's play time is mostly centered on having responsibility for a home and raising children. They have dolls, doll houses, toy cooking sets, ironing boards, vacuum cleaners, tea sets, etc. to play with which teaches them how to be responsible for a home and children at an early age. Girls (older than 20) have mothers who insisted that they learn to cook, clean, etc. so that they would be ready to accept that responsibility. Boy's play, on the other hand, involves competitive sports or games of conquest. Boys are usually given responsibility for things like taking out the trash or washing dishes and, half the time, have to be made to do that. They are not usually given responsibility for things like babysitting.

Boys who play with girls or are found playing with a doll are usually discouraged or chased to the ball field for fear of confusing their gender identity. This leaves boys at a distinct disadvantage once they become men and enter matrimony. Women go into marriage already knowing what to do with a child whereas men barely have a clue. Yet, women expect men to be immediately responsible in marriage, home making, and child rearing because they do not realize that most men have not learned or were not trained to be response able. That is, they have not learned what they need to know in order to have the ability to properly respond. We wouldn't put a 5 year old in charge of a newborn because the 5 year old is not response able or she lacks the ability to properly respond.

A person cannot be given responsibility who doesn't have response ability. We don't usually make a person responsible who is not response able. Under normal circumstances, a man would never be given responsibility who has not demonstrated that he has response ability. We would never allow a man to perform surgery on us who has not had the training and demonstrated that he has surgical ability. A man cannot be expected to be responsible for a wife, home, and children when he does not have the knowledge necessary to make him response able.

Without the knowledge to be responsible, a man will continue to lack the ability to appropriately respond. Since most men did not learn what they need to know as boys on how to be husbands and fathers, they must now learn how to be response able from their wives. Thus, women must understand what happened to their men socially and culturally, be patient, and help them develop the response ability for home and family.

Giving my book "Maximizing Fatherhood" (drwillenterprises.com) as a gift to your husband, brother, and friends will share the knowledge they need to live their lives, love their wives, and raise their children. Please DO NOT read it yourself. Just give it to the men but check to be sure that they read it.

Removing social stigmas and allowing little boys to play with dolls, with little girls, and competitive sports will help boys learn what they need to know in order to be effective fathers and husbands. Boys will learn to communicate and get along with women at an early age. Boys will also become properly prepared to handle all of their adult responsibilities by obtaining the knowledge they need to be responsible or response able.

LITTLE GIRLS SHOULD PLAY SPORTS

While little girls are playing house with baby dolls and learning to run a home, little boys are out playing competitive sports. Boys play on teams learning how to distinguish themselves as an individual while trying to achieve goals as a group. Through sports boys learn to let their physical actions and abilities speak for them. They learn that having superior physical abilities sometimes cause others to look to them for leadership. Girls, unless they have sisters close in age, largely play alone developing their imagination while directing the dolls, decorating doll houses, and managing tasks. In the process they learn to become the Chief Operations Officer of a home. Their independent play trains them to be independent and self sufficient.

This dramatic difference in playtime social development not only produces an experience gap in understanding how to manage a household it also creates a communication barrier. Little girls learn to communicate verbally as they play whereas little boys are conditioned to communicate physically. Girls learn to express themselves using words whereas boys learn to express themselves through deeds. Boys learn through sports team play to communicate without or with very few words, replacing words with signals. Give a little girl a doll and a little boy a truck, watch them play, and you will immediately see the difference. The girl will spend a lot of time talking and the boy will mostly make noises. Thus, when they grow up they will communicate differently. You will know when a woman loves you by the things she says to you. You will know when man loves you by the things he does for you. Women, therefore, use a lot of words while men utilize very few. Women communicate with each other by talking and hugging. Men communicate with each other through mostly grunts and fist bumps.

Once a man and woman get married and have to merge communication styles it causes a level of tension between them. Many couples struggle to figure out how to get their partner to understand what they are thinking and feeling. Women want to express every single one of their thoughts and feelings in 10,000 words or more. But having to absorb that much verbiage and continue to look like they're interested drives men crazy. Men only want one or two words or one or two sentences at the most to let them know what they can do. Men will listen but they are only going to listen long enough to find out what they need to do to fix the situation. They aren't really trying to understand the deep feelings your heart they just want to get to the heart of the problem so they can fix it.

Men express their thoughts and feelings in a very few words. However, receiving only a small amount of words from a man drives women crazy because they want all the details. The average woman wants to hear her man express his feelings in a way that lets her feel how he feels. This, again, drives men crazy. Communication in a relationship is the key to longevity. Men and women communicate differently so somewhere in our socialization process we must learn how the other half expresses themselves so

Relationships

that we can at least live together and be happy without driving one another crazy. If men and women could learn to understand the little things they do that drives the other crazy both would be happier. Ladies, most men who have made the commitment to marry you just want to be your husband. They don't want to be your girlfriend too and do all of the things you would do with her. If you want to do girlfriend stuff, we would rather you go out with your girlfriend. However, if we do (and it will be reluctantly) chose to go to the mall with you, please don't find a reason to make us hold your purse. Men hate that. Think about what you would do with it in that situation if we weren't there. Unless you are in trouble please don't make that high pitched squeaky voice sound. That is a type of alarm system that GOD put in a woman to alert her husband that she is in trouble. No one wants to hear a car alarm going off all the time. Men definitely don't want to hear that high pitched sound directed at them when they are in trouble. It is like scratching a nail across a chalk board.

This brings me to fighting words. People who have been together awhile know which words to use that will provoke the other to anger. Using fighting words when we are angry destroys the trust in a relationship over time. One won't want to share things with the other that might be used against them later. Men should never call their wife names and they should at all times apply the strength that GOD gave 10 men to avoid using the C word, B word, or W word against their wife at any time. It would be hard for any woman to continue to love a man who called her those names. Women should avoid at all costs using the P word, B word or any words like little or tiny relative to the D word. The word "punk" or the phrase "be a man" should be avoided at all costs as well. It is hard for a man to love a woman who does not seem to respect him.

Now, ladies, listen to what I am NOT saying. I am NOT saying that it is EVER ok under any circumstances for a man to hit a woman at any time for any reason. Do you understand that I am not saying that? Good, so now what I am about to say is intended to help women keep from inadvertently provoking a man into hitting them.

We all know that two people can engage in a fight using words. We also know that people engage in fights using their fists. GOD gave women greater verbal dexterity than men but HE gave men greater physical strength than women. When fighting with a man a woman's weapon of choice is her mouth. She utilizes her area of strength to fight with him which the man just cannot match. The woman can naturally talk circles around a man. Knowing he is out gunned, he retreats into his area of strength in battle which is his fists.

My advice here to ladies is if you are in a heated verbal fight with a man and you see him getting frustrated it is best to back off. I'm not saying this to justify a man hitting you. I'm saying this because I don't want him to hit you.

Relationships

But if you keep pressing while you see that he has become frustrated, a man who has never hit a woman before just might take a swing. I have seen guys who had never or would never hit a woman under normal circumstances get pushed over the edge. This is yet another reason why little boys and little girls should be socialized together early in their formative years.

Little boys should be allowed to play with dolls to help them learn what they need to know in order to be fathers, husbands, and to get along with women at an early age and little girls should be allowed to play competitive sports. This will help a woman understand a man's communication style and prepare her to be an effective team player within the family. Through team play a girl will learn to utilize her individual knowledge, leadership abilities, and skills to help her family achieve its goals as a unit. Sports activities will prepare a girl to lead her children to be all they can be and assist her husband in guiding them into their destiny.

Through sports play young women will learn some basic things about men that will help them in relationships. They will learn that men are competitive by nature and love to respond to a challenge. When a secure man thinks that a woman is virtuous and will be hard to get, he will rise to the challenge. An insecure man naturally hovers around a certain level, but he will also rise above his mediocre station to meet the challenge of securing a virtuous woman. However, both types of men will drop a woman whenever they discover she was only pretending to be virtuous or only playing hard to get. If a woman is all game and no glory, men will use her until they can find a real virtuous woman.

Men love it when women are direct and to the point. Sports play would condition a little girl to move from point A to point B quickly so she will know as a woman to get to the point with a man directly. Women, if you want a man to do something for you, he would like you to just tell him… period. If you want to get married, for example, you should say to your man "I want to be married by a certain date" and keep it moving. If he really wants to marry you, he will begin making preparations. But, in order to get that response you have to be direct. Ladies, if you sit around and wait until he figures it out, you will just be waiting. Oh, he will get there eventually but it is just going to take longer than if he was told directly. Every minute that you spend with a man who has no intentions of marrying you is a part of your life that you lost that you will never get back! Why waste any of your life with someone who only intends to occupy space but not take a righteous position?

In baseball, a good pitcher will try to retire as many batters as he can as early as possible so that he won't have to throw so many pitches. A woman should want to strike out as many potential suitors as she can as soon as possible. Find out early if a man has any intentions of marrying you. The quicker you know, the sooner he can go. The key is ask early and be direct. Throw that pitch fast and in the strike zone so that he can get a good hit if he wants to.

Sometimes a guy will take a good swing and miss by saying things such as "Ok, we will get married in 10 years." The wind from that swing might blow your hair back or cause your jaw to drop. However, that means he has at least given some thought to marrying you but now you can see why men probably shouldn't talk so much. In a situation where you give a man a good pitch and he just stands there with his bat on his shoulder it means he is not trying at all. He is hoping you will not see your pitch was over the plate and will let him walk on base. If you ask him if he intends to marry you and he says no, don't let him walk on base, make him walk out of your life.

Every sport has a set of rules. Men are conditioned to learn the rules of their sport and to govern themselves within the rules so that they can win. Women can take advantage of this by setting rules for their relationship that a man must govern himself by if he wants to win her. When a woman is in the process of meeting with various prospects to determine who will be her husband she must establish the rules of engagement. She must let the man that she selects know there will be no relaxing of the rules until after the engagement. A wedding occurs at the end of every good engagement. A woman has to also let a man know that, just like a quarterback has a limited time before he takes a snap and a basketball player has a limited time before he has to take a shot, there is only a limited amount of time that she will wait for him to engage.

I know that I said this before but I must repeat it again. The word "dating" is an action word that means - the act of moving toward a date. A woman must let a man know that they only begin dating after they begin moving toward a wedding date. The word DATE is an acronym that means a Divine Appointment To Edify. A DATE is not supposed to be a Doggone Attempt To Experience how a person performs in bed.

A date is a time for edification. To edify means to hold up for examination. A man usually gets serious about marrying a woman after he examines her and finds that she has all the attributes that he needs in a wife. Then he edifies her before or holds her up for examination by his family and friends. If his family and friends approve, a short time later he will present to her a ring and propose a marriage commitment. Through this process, however, a young woman has to remain firm in her position that sex will not occur until after he has given her a wedding.

Another reason why girls should play sports is so they can understand the competitive and predatory nature of men. For men who aren't seriously considering getting married dating is a competitive sport much like big game hunting. These cats, who consider themselves hunters of human prey, go out to play to see what they can catch that day. These "boys" refer to themselves as "players" or "playas" because the only thing they intend to do is play or pretend that they have feelings for you. Women who try to play games with these big boys, thinking they can use sex to make the boy give in, always lose in the end. It doesn't pay for a woman to try to play a player's game. Ladies, if you want to win, you must take my advice: Don't Play!

The reason why women always lose the player's game is because the ladies don't play to win plus they are playing a different game than men. Women play the love game whereas men play the sex game. The game women play is designed (most of the time) to lead to lasting love. The game men play is designed to get the woman in bed. Once they get her in bed they have won their game. Although women have already given up their body they are still at the beginning stage of their game. Once the woman tries to lead the man into the "serious" stage of her game, that's when the player decides to forfeit her game and leave. You see, the players want the woman's body but they place no value on it. Women give their bodies away like water but expect a man to treat her like gold. Once a woman tries to get a man to pay the high price of freedom for access to a body he's already had, he leaves and then she loses. Again, the only way for a lady to win the player's game is: don't play.

Sometimes a woman will see a guy who she thinks is worth taking the risk of playing with and getting hurt. If she concludes that she just has to try to make a play for him, then she must learn to play the sex game. However, women can't play the sex game using the man's rules. Men know the rules too well so the woman will still lose every time. Therefore, a woman must play the sex game using basketball rules. Basketball is the game that most "players" love to play. A hoop is the object a basketball player uses to score. In the sex game a player sees a woman as a basket through which to score or a hoop to shoot into (wait for it!). The net covering the bottom of a hoop is sometimes called "the panties". A young lady who decides to play the sex game must get the player to see that a wedding ring is in the shape of a hoop. She must let him know that he can take a shot at getting in the net. But she is not going to let him drive to the basket or go down low until unless he takes her to the hoop and then on to the altar!

Ladies must be aware, now, that many women have taken the risk of playing the sex game (some several times) only to end up being bitter and angry with men in general. Again, they choose to engage in the sex game with men thinking they can win while playing by the man's rules. If women want to win the sex game, they must take sex out of the game. The sex game has only one

Relationships

goal: to get the woman in bed. The sex game only has one end: the woman gets left. Therefore, a woman should not be bitter and angry with anyone but herself for choosing to get involved with a man who they know was playing the sex game. If a man doesn't make arrangements to marry a woman within about three months of meeting her but continually wants to have sex with her, he is NOT serious about being with her. He is only playing! Eventually he will try to play her off so that he can go play with someone else.

However, this is the point where women who decided to play will want this big boy to get serious. They will try to change the rules of the game once they recognize they have reached the play-offs but it will be too late. After he gets tired of playing the sex game with her, he drafts a free-agent, and then tries to play her off. The average woman becomes angry and wants to fight the new chick because she won't want to accept the fact that she lost the game in the first round of the play-offs.

Some women are good enough at the sex game to make it into the second and third round of the play-offs. That is where the man leaves her for other women and she uses her body to get him to come back two or three times. In the end, however, she never makes it to the finals. That is, she rarely if ever receives the championship ring. The women who do force their way into the finals with a player and get that ring usually only end up with a few of

Dr William Small

his children and a divorce.

Stevie Nicks of Fleetwood Mac captured, in her timeless 1977 song "Dreams", how most women feel once they realize they have reached the play-offs:

"Now there you go again

You say you want your freedom

Well who am I to keep you down

It's only right that you should play it the way that you feel it

But listen carefully to the sound of your loneliness

Like a heartbeat, drives you mad

In the stillness of remembering

What you had, and what you lost

what you had, and what you lost

Chorus:

Thunder only happens when it's raining

Players only love you when they're playing

They say, women, they will come and they will go

When the rain washes you clean you'll know"

©Nicks, Stevie, 1976, Welch Witch Music publishing

Relationships

Women who played sports as girls will recognize that a family is a lot like a football team. A football team has two leaders: a coach on the sidelines and a quarterback on the field. The coach calls the plays and the quarterback executes the plays in a precisely scripted manner that will lead the team to reach the goal. The coach and the quarterback must have the same vision on how they are going to reach that goal. The coach provides the vision and the quarterback executes the vision with precision. The husband is the coach and the wife is the quarterback. The children are the other members of the team.

While the coach provides the vision or the game plan, the game can't be played without the quarterback. Good coaches remain on the sidelines calling the plays because they know that they wouldn't do well on the field. A coach knows what a quarterback should do but he can't do what the quarterback does. That means the quarterback is the most highly prized player on the team so everyone does everything they can to protect the quarterback.

When a coach has a good quarterback he not only wants to honor him but protect him as well. He gives him everything he needs to win the game, recognizes that he is a team leader too, and never disagrees with, criticizes, or berates the quarterback in front of the other team members. The same thing is true for a husband and a wife. A good husband will honor and protect his wife as well as recognize her leadership role within the family. He will give her everything she needs to help achieve their goals. If they have disagreements those discussions are held where the children can't see or hear.

Part of the man's inherent nature is to protect his wife. If she is a good quarterback the whole team will want to protect her and place her first. Men who have a heart to honor and protect a good wife will always let her go first, place his needs and desires second to hers, open the door for her, slide out her chair, help her with her coat, and so on. Now does she really need help with her chair and coat? No. But when a man honors his wife those are some of the things that he does. It is his way of communicating his appreciation and respect for her.

A man has to be smart and tough to play football. A quarterback is a position where a player has to be very smart and tough. Most quarterbacks are tough yet they are treated as if they are the most fragile player on the team. They get treated that way because they are the most important player on the team. It is hard for a team to score or win championships without a good quarterback. But they also get treated that way because the quarterback is most vulnerable to attack. So everyone tries to protect him from sudden, vicious, or sneak attacks. While he can take a few hits, the quarterback cannot sustain a constant pounding and continue to play or stay in the game. The same is true for a woman. She is the most valuable person so she is treated like she is the most fragile player on the

Relationships

family's team. A good wife is protected because it is hard for a family to complete their vision, achieve their goals, or obtain victory without her. Therefore, the husband never hits his wife or allows her to be hit or hurt.

A wife who played sports as a girl more easily recognizes that the word TEAM is an acronym that means: Together Everybody Achieves More. Two people working together can achieve much more than one person working alone. A good sports trained wife recognizes that while the coach calls the plays from the sidelines she can call an audible (change the play) on the field. Now, she will also realize that if she has to make too many audibles either she needs a different coach or he needs a different quarterback. Ultimately either the quarterback will have to call a time-out or the coach will have to call her to the sideline to determine if she is seeing things differently or has another vision on how to reach the goal. If they disagree the coach will have to decide which vision to follow. That is because one team with two visions leads to division. Two visions (di-vison) or divided vision creates a divided course which leads to divorce. The word "divorce" is a combination of the words: divided course. Division leads to divorce when the man pursues his course and the woman is trying to pursue hers.

Therefore, knowing that it takes a unified team for a family to reach their goal, a woman who played sports as a girl will more than likely execute the plays that her coach provides. She may not agree with every play or want to do everything her husband says but she will do everything in her power to lead her family team to victory. Like the Queen that is one of the most powerful pieces in the game of Chess who could win the game on her own, a good wife allows her power to be directed by her King for the benefit of her family's kingdom.

WOMEN WHO PLAYED SPORTS HAVE BETTER SEX

A large part of a man's self-esteem is based on physical prowess or what he has the ability to do. A man's self-esteem is normally high when he can protect and provide for his family. His self-esteem soars when he can do those and satisfy his wife sexually. Men take a lot of pride in what they can do and most men take pride in knowing or believing that they know how to satisfy their wives sexually.

Now, most women know that there are men who know how to satisfy a woman sexually and there are those who only think they know. The guys who know understand that they must make love to their wife's body and mind at the same time. The men who don't know focus on one or two parts of a woman's body and they jump around like a kid in a bouncy house. The men who know what to do most often listened and learned from women or other men who know what to do. A lot of men who don't know what to do don't want to be told by women what to do. Insecurity or low self-esteem causes them to complain or feel offended when a woman tries to give them instructions on how to satisfy her. They have a standard routine that they use with every woman because they believe that it will satisfy any woman. Their pride prevents them from learning how to satisfy their wife. Thus, their wives have to lie about their ability to satisfy and are reduced to making sounds and faking orgasms just to get their husbands off of them as quickly as possible.

Sports trained women know how to motivate an underperforming team mate to be better without berating or making them feel bad. Sports trained women have better sex because they know how to guide their underperforming husband into giving them what they need to be satisfied. These women understand how to explain to a man that achieving the female orgasm is not an individual sport but rather requires a team effort. The man has to listen to what his wife wants him to do and then do it when and the way she wants it done. After a while she won't have to tell him what to do, he will just pick up the signals she gives her sports fan and then do what he knows that she likes when she likes it.

Good sex requires good communication. This is similar to the communication between a pitcher and a catcher. The catcher uses his hand to send the pitcher a signal or instruction from between his legs. That signa tells the pitcher what type of pitch and where in relation to home plate he should throw it. If a pitcher does not agree with that signal, he will shake his head as if to say no. When a woman, who is like a catcher, sends the man a signal on what to do to satisfy her, he can't be like the pitcher and shake his head or say no. He has to deliver the pitch how, when, and where she wants it. If she wants it left, right, low and deep into center, or in the upper deck, he has to know her signals and deliver. It is in the man's best interest to work with his wife during sex, like a good pitcher and catcher, because it will make her want to strike out any other man who tries to step to the plate.

Contrary to what some men think women know their physical equipment better than men. There have been many studies and surveys where women report not being able to achieve an orgasm inner vaginally while having no problem achieving an orgasm externally. This is only proves that women know what to do and a lot of men don't have a clue. To be fair, just like impotence with some men is a psychological condition rather than physical malfunction, not being able to have an orgasm inner vaginally is psychological for some women. Women who have been abused sexually or who were conditioned to believe that sex is dirty and the pleasure of it makes them feel guilty often report not being able to or have never experienced an inner vaginal orgasm. Some women aren't comfortable with their bodies and that causes them to be inhibited. Then some women who are on the verge of orgasm feel like they have to pee so they hold it back. These women can have an inner vaginal orgasm if they first have the right man who they can guide and if they just relax, lose their inhibitions, and "let" it happen.

A man who knows what to do will know that whether or not the female orgasm will occur is not up to him rather it is up to her based on what is happening in her mind. Orgasms, whether male or female, always begin in the mind. A woman could normally enjoy having sex with her husband but not have an orgasm sometimes because too many things are on her mind; things that happened that day, things she has to do the next day, and so on. A man who wants complete access to a woman's body at night has to begin making love to her mind during the day. Then when it comes time for making love, she has already had the night on her mind all day. Therefore, she will put aside all other concerns from her mind and allow herself to become mentally and physically engrossed in the pleasure of making love.

When men who don't know what to do find out that a woman has not had an orgasm they take it as a personal challenge. They embark upon a quest to "make" her have an orgasm but it never happens because they don't know what to do. Men who do know what to do will view it as a time for patience, communication, and guidance. These men understand that they may have to teach their wives some things, particularly if she feels inhibited by the very act of sex. He may have to teach her, for example, what the Bible says about it: "Marriage is honorable in all and the [my note: marital] bed undefiled but whoremongers [my note: those who seek prostitutes] and adulterers [my note: those who cheat] GOD will judge (Hebrew 13:4)."

Women who feel inhibited by the act of sex must understand that there is nothing that is dishonorable before GOD in sex between a husband and wife. Whatever they do in the marital bed is not considered defilement, dirty or filthy in HIS eyes. The only thing that is actually defilement between a married couple is that which feels like a defilement to either one of them. If a woman doesn't want to do certain things because it would make her feel defiled afterward, her husband must respect the way she feels. Sometimes women will want to put things places in a man where no real man would ever want it to go. So she must then respect the way that her husband feels.

"…to avoid fornication, let every man have his own wife and let every woman have her own husband. Let the husband render due benevolence [my note: from the Greek word "eunoia" which means wholehearted, eager, respectful sexual submission]: and likewise also the wife unto the husband. The wife hath not power of her own body, but the husband: and likewise also the husband hath not power of his own body but the wife. Defraud not one another except it be with consent for a time that you may give yourselves to fasting and prayer; and come together again, that satan tempt you not for your incontinency (1 Corinthians 7:2-5)."

The urge to have sex is a natural urge that GOD placed in our bodies so that we would fulfill HIS command to "be fruitful and multiply". HE created the institution of marriage so that men and women can fulfill this obligation and so that their union and the fruit of it can be blessed. The urge for sexual intercourse is powerful and nearly impossible to resist when we continually have close contact with the opposite sex. So GOD instructs us here, to avoid fornication or having sex out of wedlock, a man and woman should get married. Then HE tells us that it is our duty to submit to our spouse sexually (in every case eagerly and respectfully) whenever they want us to. So when a wife grabs her husband by the collar and says "I want it now, boy" he has to eagerly submit his body to her. His body is not his to withhold from her, his body belongs to her. GOD considers withholding one's body from their spouse an act of fraud that gives satan room to meddle in their marriage and tempt one of them to go outside of the marriage. Sexual fraud could cause dissolution of the marriage.

Sports trained women understand the need for sex in a man and know how to utilize sex to keep her team intact. She knows that her orgasms will only be as good as her ability to guide her mind and her man into achieving orgasmic victory. A man is going to get his, but working together will make her able to sing the Star Spangled Banner like Whitney. The difference being that she won't have to fake singing and the sounds won't need to be pre-recorded. Sports trained women recognize that the right to have frequent orgasms is coded into the US Constitution: "We hold these truths to be self-evident, that all men are created equal, that they are endowed by their Creator with certain unalienable rights that among these are life, liberty and really good sex with one's spouse..." While all men are created equal and all men are endowed, all men have not been trained equally and all men are not equally endowed. Sports trained women understand how to train a man to be "her" man so that she doesn't get treated like his last chick. She will also know how to train her man on how to utilize the equipment that he was endowed with her in a manner that will lead him to always get a good hit.

Relationships

Chapter 8
WHY IS IT HARD TO FIND LOVE?

"True love is like a pair of socks; you gotta have two and they've gotta match." ~ Keith Sweat

According to the 2000 US Census, 53% of all American homes are headed by single mothers. Many national polls have revealed that when asked whether they would rather be single and dating or happily married, the average person, both male and female, chooses marriage. Examining these statistics caused the question to linger in my mind for an answer: If there are so many unmarried people out there who want to be married, why do they find it difficult to find someone that they would love to be in love with?

I even looked at the rolls of average sized churches and found that, for the most part, 50% or more of their members are single or divorced. With all of the unmarried and divorced people in church that would like to be married it seems there should be more weddings in the church! What is preventing people who want to be married from getting together that are going to church every week together? I believe it is because they have learned to be leery or frightened of one another. While they go to church together, they never really get to know each other and consequently grow fearful of one another. Fear can no more grow into love than an apple can grow into an orange.

People who are fearful of one another cannot grow to love as long as they retain that fear. The bible says that perfect love casts out fear. In order for two people that had been fearful of one another to grow to love each other, one of them has to decide to overcome their fear and take the risk of trying to get to know the other person. After one of them extends an offering of love to the other consistently, it will cast the fear out of the other one suddenly.

Fear comes as the result of a lack of knowledge. It is hard to find love in many cases because people who don't know each other are fearful of approaching someone they don't know. Those who have been in painful relationships previously tread much too fearfully when seeking a new relationship. The least little thing about the new person that reminds them of the previous person makes them run for the safety of singleness but keeps them in the state of lonely and looking. They would really rather be in a loving relationship but convince themselves that they would be better off single than have to put up with what they endured previously. It may be hard for average people to find love but those in this category make it unduly hard on themselves to find love. They would be advised to continue to be cautious but to give people more of a chance, using perhaps a three strike rule, if they really want to find love.

Fear of rejection is another big inhibitor to finding love for some people. The pain of rejection makes them fearful to approach or try to meet someone who they don't know. Whenever you approach someone to get to know them and they reject you that could actually be a positive in some cases not a negative. The rejection is an immediate acknowledgement that they are not the one for you. You just saved a lot of time, energy, and possibly money by learning immediately that this person was not right for you. This makes you free to find someone who is really interested in you rather than being tied up trying to make them love you.

Anger may be the greatest factor that keeps men and women from getting together and/or staying together. Bring up the topic of male and female relationships in a public forum and you will immediately see that women are angry. The majority of women complain that they cannot seem to find men who are real men. Women have to deal with men coming into a relationship who are not prepared to carry their weight. Women want men who can give them security but what they find are men who are still trying to deal with issues left over from former lovers and their mothers which they should have gotten over a long time ago. They come to women acting as if they are in a state of becoming, trying hard to make it, and expecting the woman to give them support to reach their goal. When women take the risk and give them love, emotional and financial support these men either cheat or run off with another woman in the end. The men often leave women with babies that she didn't have when he showed up thus leaving her distressed financially and the babies in poverty.

In some cases, when women ask a man who is not carrying his weight to step up the pace of his progress he will lash out almost as if he hates her. He will demand respect as a man from this woman with whom he has been living but not supporting. In reality, Uncle Sam is her man. Uncle Sam has been providing the financial support she needs to have a place to live via section 8 and meals to eat through food stamps. Through those and other subsidies such as those that provide no or low cost gas and electricity, Uncle Sam is paying the bills in the home. However, this big boy demands the respect that a man should get even while he doesn't do anything that a woman would expect a respectable man to do. Because he lashed out she often has to call the police to have him put out.

The experience that women have had with men like this causes many of them to run to the other extreme from being a helper to wanting to be helped. As a result of past experiences many women want marriage to be a service agreement wherein a man provides them with physical, emotional, and financial security. They want a man to have something or to be able to do something for them. When women find men who both have and can do something for them these relationships fail also. Given the fact that they gave so much in the previous relationship and got burned, they determine to give little or nothing in this relationship. When a person is looking for someone to do something for them with no intent to provide reciprocity there is no economic or spiritual practicality to that marriage or relationship. It cannot flourish under those conditions therefore they fail. However, having another man walk away causes women to become even angrier. The sorry men have to be chased away and the good men seem to just walk away.

When I listen to women talk to their girlfriends, they unfairly assign all of the blame for the failure of relationships to the man. At the same time women don't want to hear any criticism whatsoever directed at them. Women have had to put up with so much that they tend to recoil whenever they are criticized by men. However, in relationships like the one outlined above, the woman wanted the man to have and do everything while she just be. She seems to have forgotten that her previous relationship didn't work because the man used her in that same manner. I often hear women say "A man is going to have to just accept me as I am." At the same time, they want that man have and do everything with no intention of doing anything themselves except be. They get angry because the men won't just accept them as they are in a

Relationships

relationship without reciprocity. Then the chasm between men and women continues to deepen.

When men try to have a discussion with women about relationships and they try to assign ANY of the blame to women or try to get them to accept any of the responsibility, there is a nuclear explosion. Women want men to hear loud and clear that they are angry. Men have to deal with a war-like hostility that comes from the female section when relationship issues are raised. Men seem to be confused as to why women are angry. Seeing that men are ignorant to their anger nearly drives women crazy. It also frustrates women that they don't regularly have an opportunity to fully express the anger that they feel. Once they get a chance to let some of their anger out the men respond by trying to let the women know that they are angry and frustrated too. That is like throwing gasoline on a fire so men invoke even more anger in those women. If most men had the ability to listen to women long enough attentively, they would see the anger women express appears to rise up from their soul or spirit and is deeply imbedded in the hearts of many women. Men are the source of much of their anger but some of it also appears related to the pressures women have to deal with in society.

American society forced women to fight for the right to be equal with men who largely do not present themselves as men. The boy like antics and tactics in the work place are largely offensive to female sensibilities. Men are often hostile or insensitive to women on the job and their need to balance work, family, and caring for elderly parents. Women realize that most men in the work place are married or have a mother yet they seem oblivious and rather hostile to women as if they hold a personal grudge against women in general.

Some women are angry because they believe the very least men should do is protect women. There have been many reports where women have been attacked in public, men stood by and watched, but no one came to their rescue. The most dangerous place for a woman is the home. FBI statistics reveal that a white woman is more likely to be killed by her husband or son than any strange black man on the street. The same is true for black and Hispanic women but the culprit us usually a current or former lover. At the same time, black and Hispanic women are going to jail today in record numbers trying to support the men they love who are involved in various types of crime. The very least that women expect in return for the love and support they give men is protection. They are angry that they don't get it especially when they find that the man who they supported in crime was willing to testify against them to reduce his time.

Another factor that prevents men and women from getting together is a lack of knowledge. Both men and women appear to be unaware of the little things that could cause someone to reject them immediately. There is a thin line between confidence and arrogance and a big difference between being assertive and aggressive. Women love men who are confident but loathe men that are arrogant. Men develop interest in women who are assertive but detest women that are aggressive. Ladies, if you don't know already, aggressiveness in one's career or investments is different from aggressiveness in relationships, please don't confuse the two. Aggressiveness in careers and investments comes from confidence that one is good at what they do or a belief that they are betting on a sure thing. Aggressiveness in relationships makes a woman appear desperate or easy. The underlying cause of arrogance in men and aggressiveness in women in the pursuit of love is a low level of self esteem. Men with low self esteem are usually rejected outright and women with low self esteem are usually used for sex and then rejected. However, the pain of repeated rejection also makes them fearful of approaching or trying to meet someone who they don't know.

Those who know their self esteem is low and who know they have a fear of being rejected must first seriously consider therapy to improve their total sense of well being before they attempt to enter into a relationship. Anyone who does not feel good about themselves cannot be good for anyone else. Once they are healed of whatever caused their condition and begin to love themselves, they will be ready to find someone else to love them as well.

It is hard for many otherwise healthy people to find love because no one ever taught them the techniques that have worked for other people. Using some or all of the following techniques will help healthy people find a happy loving relationship:

Network – The standard rule to remember when trying to find love is that everyone in life is connected to someone else in some way. Therefore, if you want to meet someone and you are shy or afraid of scaring them by being aggressive, find someone who knows them that can introduce you to them .We are only three people away from anybody who we don't know. There is always somebody we know who knows somebody that knows the person we want to know. Tap into your social network to find out who knows the person, learn more about them, and find someone who can introduce you to them. In business we need contacts to get contracts and we need to network to get work. The same process can be utilized when looking for love.

Set A Standard – To find the right person that we want and to avoid getting involved with the kind of person we don't requires setting a standard. You have to know the type of person that will be right for you: educationally, socially and financially. Learn to only engage those types of persons and don't settle. Women looking for love have the hardest time maintaining a standard. They often settle for who's available or get pressured by their friends to do

Relationships

so. If their standard is rich men, they fear being called a gold digger if they only date rich men. If a rich man is what you like, don't let friends pressure you into a relationship with a garbage man. That is, unless you know he just hit the lottery. He may look good and the sex may be great but in the long run you will not be satisfied.

Most women in this situation will settle for the garbage man who is available and then try to pressure him to become rich. The problem here is if it was in the man's nature to be rich, he would already be well on his way to becoming rich. His woman would not have to push or prod him to execute a plan to become rich. Water always seeks its own level. A person that is on the 10th rung of the ladder of success who meets someone who is on the 4th rung and tries to pull them up may have some success at getting them to move up a rung or two initially. However, they will sink back down to the 4th rung eventually if they don't develop the skills required to remain on the 10th. But they will blame their failure on their partner.

If a man already has the tools and gifts to be rich in him, a woman can help push him reach that goal. But if a man does not have the tools and gifts, a woman should not try to make him be something he is not equipped to become. Nothing good ever comes out of a female made man. A man has to be his own man in order for him to be any good for a woman. A man cannot take a woman from the ghetto, pull her out of poverty, and expect her to act like royalty. The key to becoming what one wants to be is in thinking and acting like they already are. If a woman had not already learned to think and act like royalty on her own mentally, while she yet lives in the ghetto, she will eventually find a way to fall back into or remain connected to the ghetto. Therefore, set the standard for the type of man or woman that you want and don't settle for a fixer upper.

You Get Where You Go – Persons of the same social status usually travel in the same circles and frequent the same places. Once you set a standard, you must know where the person you would like to meet likes to go to interact with others socially. The rule to remember here is you get where you go. If you go to neighborhood bars where auto workers frequent, you will more than likely meet an auto worker.If you go to exclusive clubs where millionaires frequent, you are more than likely to meet a millionaire. The people you will get to meet will depend on the places you go. If you want to meet an auto worker, you have to go where auto workers go.

Numbers Game – This technique is the simplest yet the most scientific. A man who wants to have a very attractive wife has to set that standard and don't settle. Otherwise, he will eventually make some woman who he does not see as attractive as he would want her to be very unhappy. The rule that this man must remember is acquiring the type of person that one wants is based on the law of inevitability, which is also known as the numbers game. A man who wants a very attractive wife must only ask out very attractive women. The law of inevitability dictates that if he determines to ask nothing but attractive women for dates, one of them will inevitably say yes. Those who are persistent in pursuing the type of person that they want can always achieve their goal if they remember to consistently apply this rule. Don't abuse someone by letting them be Mr. or Ms. Right now while you are waiting for Mr. or Ms. Right to come along. That will create a karmic debt that you will have to repay. When you think you have found Mr. or Ms. Right, they will in turn use you as Mr. or Ms. Right now.

Conduct Job Interviews – To do this successfully requires good listening skills and discipline. A life in love is not just a love affair, it is also a business arrangement. Your business affairs will be merged with the person whom you love. The person you love will have to be able to do business. Therefore, you must conduct an interview as you are trying to get to know that person to see if they are qualified to handle the job. If you have a stubborn personality, there are certain persons who you will match in compatibility. Conduct an interview to see if that person can handle you. Every employer has a set of questions and knows the answers that he or she expects to receive to determine if a person will be right for the job. Know what you will need your partner to do and be prepared to conduct a job interview.

Plan The Work And Work The Plan – Now that you understand the rules that others have used to find love, you have to devise a plan to find love. The rules will all work, but only if you put them to work. Therefore, plan your work and work your plan and you will be able to find your perfect woman or man.

Finally, some people get caught up in waiting for GOD to send them a mate. This is a false faith exercise that leaves people lonely and looking. GOD will not send you a specific person to marry because that would violate your free will. HE puts several good people in your path and allows you to pick the one you want. Anyone who loves you would want you to be free to make your own choices and not restrict you to what they think is right for you. GOD is love so HE always gives you the freedom to choose.

DOES THE CHRUCH PLAY A ROLE?

A debate breaks out occasionally as to whether or not the church plays a role in making it hard to find love. This answer is difficult for some to decide or discern as a result of cognitive dissonance that exists within the people who regularly attend church. The church members know, along with those that are ministers and/or relatives of pastors and ministers, that in some ways it is true that the church is keeping women single and we know in some ways the people are doing it to themselves.

Relationships

Understanding that those two things are partially TRUE places those who want to find love or find the answer to why some have a hard time finding love in the proverbial catch-22. This dissonance freezes their mind in a position of inaction and causes it to fail to do what is necessary to change the condition or get free. Then the pastor comes along and excuses their inaction by saying "Don't worry about all of the negativity that you see in the church. Just focus on worshipping GOD." Now, the church members are relieved of the responsibility of taking action or doing something to correct all of the negativity that they see.

I have been in church all of my life. I begged to be baptized at age 5. I have circled the globe nearly twice and attended as well as taught in churches all over the world. I have seen firsthand that there is some merit to the argument that the church is keeping some women single.

I constantly hear young Christian men say that they are a man of GOD "looking" for a woman of GOD "in" Christ. So I have to ask them how long have you been looking and why is she so hard to find in church? If GOD knew you were looking for a wife (I assume you prayed and asked HIM) why did HE send you to a church where your wife was not already waiting? You see, their point appears to confirm the position of some that the church is somehow keeping people who want to be married single. I don't know if what the leaders do is an error of the head or the heart but I have seen some of the things they do that either purposely or subconsciously keeps people from getting together. Sometimes, as a result of knowing how this is going to affect these people lives I almost want to cry.

The majority of people who attend church on any given Sunday are single, widowed or divorced. If you ask them, most of them would say that they'd rather be married. So, with all of those people coming together every week who want to be married, why is it so hard for them to get together? The problem is the pastor! He can SEE that he is conducting more funerals each month than marriages yet it seems that he/she rarely tries to do anything about it. The question is why? I don't think it will be easy to get to the truth of the matter because everybody has been conditioned (like a cult member) to lie and say their pastor does do whatever is said that pastors don't do that will help people find love among the members of their church. Everybody's pastor encourages them to get married and is doing everything to cause more weddings in their church let THEM tell it.But if you go in their churches you will never SEE it. This knee jerk response wherein people are readily willing to lie and throw away their character and integrity to lie for their pastor is a telling show of the mental hold he/she has on the people.

Black women in particular must come to cold reality and face the economic fact that it is in your pastor's best interest to keep you single. Now, whether or not he is actively doing that, only you really know. However, you must be made aware that you have more money and more time to devote to your pastor and his vision when you are single. Once you get married he will have to share you with your family, more particularly your husband. Your husband and family are going to consume a lot more of your time and finances. Therefore, he periodically instructs the women to "watch out" for people who come to church looking for a mate. He instructs you to "wait" until GOD "sends" you a mate when he knows or should know that instruction is not biblically sound. Yet women believe him because they've been trained to love him.

Since the women are so thoroughly trained to love their pastor they have difficulty finding a real man to love them. A real man will not want to get involved with a woman who is already in love with another man. That last thing that a real man wants is another man's woman. It is an insult to a man who you want to marry to stand to receive approval from your de-facto husband. A real man is not going to do it yet this is what your pastor instructs you to do. You must bring your man to him for approval.

If he won't come, then you won't receive your pastor's blessing. A real man is not going to want a woman who allows another man to influence her in that way. He knows that he will have difficulty winning her heart and mind because it already belongs to her pastor. These are the games that pastors play with women that keeps them from being eligible to marry real men. Therefore, church going women end up with weak men, a man who is fighting with addiction, struggling to remain free from prison, or struggling to find a job. Pastors love for women to be with men like these because the trouble they will go through with these men will keep them coming to church. Ergo, most church women continue to remain lonely and looking.

When I hear women say they are waiting for GOD to send them a husband I have to tell them that their belief is borne out of BAD religious teaching. The Bible says on the seventh day GOD rested. HE made creation, did all that HE was going to do, and then sat down. This means that GOD has already made many people who would be GOOD for us to marry. It is our job now to pick the one we want. If GOD did the picking, it would violate our free will. GOD has given us authority and dominion over the earth and the Holy Spirit resident within us to give us power to choose right over wrong or good over evil.

Yet, we are taught by most pastors that we are powerless, they are the ones with authority, they are the ones who are anointed, and that we have to come to them in order to hear from GOD! Only a cult leader would think and speak like that. There is only one head and only one leader in the body of Christ. All the rest of us, including the pastors and ministers, are brothers and sisters in Christ. The rest of us make up the Body of Christ. GOD is not interested in creating authoritarian leaders in the context of a religious body. GOD is interested in creating strong families as a unified body.

The family is the foundation of the church. The GODHEAD, the Eloheim, is a family unit. GOD organized a family unit in the Garden of Eden where HE mated all the animals together. When Adam asked for a helper, GOD built him a wife simply because there was no suitable mate for him among the animals.

However, this is the example preachers use to support their theory that GOD will send us a mate. No, all of the mates that GOD is going to make HE has already made. GOD has already placed you where a person who would be good for you can come into your view. That is, HE has already sent you. Now the rest is up to you. You have to pick one from among those in your presence and decide if they would be good for you. If GOD gave you the ability to think, discern and decide but you have to go to a preacher to ask if a person is the right one for you, then apparently have no relationship with GOD. If you are doing what GOD said and you are allowing the Holy Spirit to guide you into all truth, why do you need a man to tell you what to do? It is because you have been conditioned to remain dependent upon man.

This is the reason so many people who go to church together can't seem to get together. Some pastors even emphatically teach that a person should not come to church looking for a spouse. Why? If a spouse is what we want why not try to find him or her among GOD's children? Where else should we go? WHY would GOD not want HIS church to be a place where one who loves HIM could find a spouse who also loves HIM? Was not the Garden of Eden the first church or place where man worshipped GOD? Did not Adam and Eve find each other in the garden? Telling you not to look for a mate in the same place where you are supposed to find GOD, but rather to WAIT for GOD to send you one, is a form of confusion. GOD is not the author of confusion! Therefore, you won't find the Spirit of the Living GOD in that instruction.

The reason why GOD would rather you to be married is because HE charged mankind to be fruitful and multiply. You cannot be fruitful, which means to bear children, except within the family context. GOD said in Deuteronomy 8:18 "I have given you power to get wealth..." Wealth was designed by GOD to be developed within the family context. In biblical days the more children a man had the wealthier he was. In Deuteronomy 8:18 GOD said "I have given you power to get wealth." That power resides in the productivity and potential of his wife and children. If a man understands how to recognize and utilize his wife and children's gifts, talents, and abilities as designed by GOD to produce wealth for their family collectively, the blessings will overtake them (Deuteronomy 28:2). If he works the principles that make his children productive, they will work to make him prosper. Richard Williams, father of Venus and Serina, as well as Joe Jackson understood. While there may be a good/evil contrast between the two, they both worked the principle and it worked to make their children productive and them prosperous.

The prosperity preachers who strive to keep the people in their church single don't seem to understand that a strong family is a prosperous family. If you have strong families, you will have strong and prosperous churches as well as strong and prosperous communities. While they preach prosperity, most of these pastors do not seem to understand how to build strong churches. They spend little to no time teaching their members how to build strong families (yes, I already know that your preacher does). Yet, this is what they should be doing all of the time. They should be teaching the people of the church about being strongly committed to GOD within the context of being strongly committed to family.

The preachers pervert that message by making the church emblematical of a family rather than building on strong families. They will call their churches the "this" family or the "that" family. Families were designed to multiply and prosper through the act of intercourse. They engage their church to join them in a path to prosperity through a type of intercourse. That is, they give the people their vision and set them on their course as the head or husbandman of this church family. The women were designed by GOD go give birth to the vision. However, there are some men in the church who try to assume the task of giving birth to the vision as well. Then these same preachers act like they can't figure out why they get caught in adultery. They act like they have no clue as to why there is so much adultery, fornication and homosexuality going on in and among the church.

The purpose of a family is to worship GOD by multiplying or having children and prospering. After salvation this is the only message that a pastor should teach or preach. He or she has to set the people on a course of fulfilling GOD's vision not his or hers. In doing so, the preacher will make the people, their families, the church, and the surrounding community to prosper. Then, the people will be able to freely worship GOD, fulfilling HIS first commandment (be fruitful and multiply), through marrying and the giving of marriage.

Relationships

Chapter 9
AVOID ATTRACTING ABUSIVE MEN

"No man is worth your tears, but once you find one that is, he won't make you cry." ~ William James

When a woman says that she does not need a man, what she just expressed is an incomplete statement. The average woman knows that she needs a man but she just doesn't need they type of man that she is used to dealing with. If you ask a liberated woman if she needs a man she will say "I don't NEED a man but I would like help sometimes taking care of this house, paying the bills, and taking care of these kids. But, no, I don't need a man." What they are actually saying is I want a man but I don't need to put up with the crap that the men in my life have made me have to deal with. Therefore, I want to give women who want to have a good man information on how to avoid attracting the same type of man that they don't need over and over again.

Now, this chapter is probably going to create controversy. What I am about to share causes some women to claim that I am blaming the victim when in reality I am trying to prevent women from becoming victims. There are certain things that attract abusive men to certain women that are not necessarily due to who they are but rather what they do and where they go. Women who do not know what these things are should at least be made aware of them. They can then choose whether or not to use the information to protect themselves, their sisters, and their girlfriends.

If there was a rash of women being raped on a college campus, for example, we would warn them not to do certain things that might make them vulnerable to attack. We might warn them not to walk alone at night when the rapist is targeting women who are walking alone at night. But if a woman was raped after being warned not to walk alone at night, it would not be blaming the victim if another warning was issued to other women not to walk alone at night. That would be an attempt to prevent those women from making the same mistake and making themselves vulnerable to attack. The subsequent warning would not be an attempt to blame the woman for being raped.

So, when it comes to the area of domestic abuse, if women do certain things that makes them vulnerable to either approach or attack by an abusive man, some women say that I should not say that certain actions makes women vulnerable because it is akin to blaming the victim. However the difference between me and them is I have conducted extensive research in the area of domestic abuse and have counseled hundreds of men and women who were chronic abusers and chronically abused. In my experience, both the abuser and the abused have a distinct behavior pattern that makes it easy to identify them as such.Abusive men seem to know this which is why they seem to know which women to target. They love to select women who have been abused before which is the reason why some women seem to fall into one abusive relationship after another with one abusive man after another. Men who are abusers know how to identify a woman who is vulnerable to being abused or who is already conditioned to put up with their crap.

All abusers and all those being abused, do the exact same things while they are engaged in the abusive relationship. If they all do the same things while in the relationship, there must be something that they all do to get themselves into the relationship in the first place. Haven't you ever wondered why certain women seen to fall into one abusive relationship after another? Doesn't it make sense that there is something that they are doing that gets them there. If we could identify what the behaviors are that lead women into abusive relationships, wouldn't you want to educate all women on what those behaviors are? We could then probably protect some women and their children from being abused.

All abusive men, bar none, know how to select a woman who is vulnerable to abuse. All abused women, bar none, particularly the chronically abused, do and say exactly the same things to get themselves selected. Most of us know that abused women become chronically abused because they refuse to leave the man after the first instance of abuse. Everyone knows they should leave, but the abuse continues and yet they won't leave.

Some do leave but true to their behavior pattern, too many of them go back at some point. Most chronically abused women find a way to blame themselves for their abuser's behavior. They may have their abuser arrested but too often they drop the charges. We have all seen or know of women that were being abused who have done these things. So, is it blaming the victim if we warn other women not to do these things? Wouldn't it help to make them and their children safer if we did warn them?

Women need to know that all abusive men do and say the same things to lure a woman into a relationship and trap her in it. It as if someone has written an abuser's handbook and they are all working from the same game plan. Women have to understand that an abusive man can be very charming, funny, and cute because he has boy-like qualities but he is dangerous. Once an abusive man tells a woman that he is going to kill her, it is not a matter of whether or not he will kill her at that point it is just a matter of when.

The average abusive man's psychological problem is he hates his mother. The lack of time, attention, affection, or emotional availability by their mommies leaves abusive men with a need to control the women in their lives because they could not control their mothers. This is why they will beat a woman up and then make her hug them. The hate they feel for women is related to how they feel their mother treated them. Many were rarely hugged and often left alone or cast aside while she cared for a man that they did not like. A lot of these men caught their mothers in the midst of having sex while they were young boys. Thus, they develop a deep seated hatred for other women who appear to be easy or sexually promiscuous. Therefore, they love to abuse women who give in too quickly to them sexually.

Most abusers know that they cannot take their frustration out on their mothers so they take it out on someone who reminds them of their mother. I hear too many women say "The way to know how a man will treat you is seeing how he treats is mother." Ladies, never follow that dangerous line of thought ever again. Don't be fooled by the fact that a man appears to really love his mother. An abusive man will dote on his mother because he is still struggling to get her attention and affection. All abusers learn to be very loving, charming and manipulative as a means of winning their mother's attention and affection. However, they hate the fact that they basically had to con their mothers into loving them. It appears to them that their mothers had no feelings for them so they develop a lack of empathy for the pain of others. Thus, they can be a very warm and affectionate boy one minute and extremely violent monster the next.

Relationships

While they lavish affection on their moms lovingly periodically they will get very angry with her. That, ladies, is a warning sign to leave that guy alone. Eventually he will be taking the anger he has for her out on you.

Abusers all have a Dr Jekyll and Mr. Hyde type split personality. The women whom they abuse fall in love with the loving, sweet, and charming Dr Jekyll but Mr. Hyde is a monster who has both homicidal and suicidal tendencies. The abuser's basic profile is they all have boy like qualities, are all needy, and in some ways appear helpless which makes them attractive to women who need to be needed. However, whenever you encounter a grown man with these qualities, ladies, I advise you to run as far and as fast you can to get away from him.

Some of the abuser's common behaviors include: apologizing and romancing their victims after a violent episode and vowing not to do it again but they always do it again. Abusers all find various ways to blame the abused for getting abused. All abusers have sex with more than one woman but they all have one woman who reminds them of their mothers that they want to control. All abusers have an uncanny ability to impregnate the women whom they want to control. They pressure these women or manipulate them into having unprotected sex for the purpose of getting them pregnant. The pregnancy, in their mind, will make her unavailable sexually to other men while they are out with other women. The children will keep her busy and limit her ability to keep track of his activities.

Abusers manipulate their children into becoming emotionally dependent on them by lavishing attention, affection, and treats on them. They subtly train the children to disobey their mother and make it hard for her to make them mind so she will need him to help her.

Every time she tries to break away from him, he uses the children as a means to maintain contact with and control over her. These are not things that some abusers do. These are things they all do.

So, you see from just a few examples that abusers and the abused have distinct behavior patterns. Now we need to know the behaviors that cause women to fall into abusive relationships. These behaviors alert abusive men that these ladies are in a position to be or are vulnerable to being abused. My goal here is to help women avoid being attracted by and attracted to men with abusive personalities. If warning women that there are certain behaviors that other women have engaged in that made them attractive to abusive men makes me appear to be blaming the victim, then that is the risk I have to take to help provide women with the knowledge they need to protect themselves. The feminists can get angry with me if they want but I don't care.

Relationships

Ladies, one or more of the following very simple behaviors cause women to be attractive to an abusive man:

- allowing a man to come into their lives because they needed to have the attention or affection of a man
- letting a man take the lead in a relationship without taking any responsibility for where it goes
- working and making their own money but either dating or living with a man who neither works nor has his own money
- allowing a man to come to their home within a week or two of meeting him
- having sex with a man within a short time of meeting him
- having unprotected sex with a man they barely knew
- frequently going out with a group of women and always being the one in the group who enters or leaves the room last
- being the one who always has to find an extra chair for the table in a night club
- having a father who abused her mother

Every woman must understand that abusive men are like predatory animals therefore women must always be sober and vigilant in public. Vigilant means to stand guard, watching for the approach of the enemy. The adversary, as a roaring lion, is walking about seeking women who will allow him to devour them. He knows when you are ripe for attack, ladies, by the things you do and the places you go. An abusive man operates on predatory instincts so he knows by instinct which women to attack. His favorite places to hunt for victims are places where it is socially acceptable to offer a woman alcohol or other things that will lower her inhibitions and make her more susceptible to his charms.

The abusive man's predatory behavior most closely resembles the lion. A lion roams and crouches about seeking to identify which animal in a herd that he will select for lunch. A lion usually chooses to attack one of the animals that are either at the back of the pack or one that is not paying attention. This one gets caught simply because she was the last in line, unaware of, or slow to recognize that the lion was a threat.

Just like the lion, an abusive man watches various women or groups of women in an effort to see which woman is the most vulnerable or which one is not paying attention as he goes on the prowl. In a nightclub setting, for example, the predatory man watches as groups of women enter the room. He observes to see which ones come in last. If there are more than four of them, he watches to see which one goes to find the extra chair. (A woman said to me "I do this all the time but I'm not vulnerable" but then I found out that she had been dealing with one abusive man after another since she first began dating. You may think that this doesn't apply to you, but I am simply telling you what predatory men look for. If they try to capture you, you may be able use this knowledge to escape.) Then, he waits to catch that woman alone, watching the coats or purses of the other ladies while they go to dance. After the others take off he will attempt to capture her or cut her out of the group.

A predator who is really cleaver and/or cute will wait until the other ladies come back before asking her to dance or attempting to cut her out of the group. He will do this because he understands that this woman may not be feeling positive about herself. She can sense that she may be the low person in the group. So she will do things to make it appear to the other women that she is indifferent to being in that position. Therefore, he knows that she may not accept his invitation to dance while she is alone because she feels obligated to watch everyone's things. Plus, she will want to make the other women believe that she didn't want to dance anyway. If she is not feeling really good about herself, she is also likely to try to make him feel bad about himself by rejecting him. She will do this because misery loves company and hurting people tend to hurt other people. So his tactic will be to just talk with her while the others are away.

His goal, in this situation, is to get her phone number. He has to get her to let her guard down so must make her laugh, keep her amused, and make her feel pretty. He needs her phone number because knows that he will need to talk to her privately before he can lure her into a sexual relationship. He may be the type that she wouldn't give a second look. However, predators have a high level of charm and an uncanny ability in the art of amusement. Charm and humor are the main weapons the abusive men use to get women to lower their guard. I cringe every time I hear a woman say "A sense of humor is important in a man. He has to make be laugh."

The power in charm is to make a woman disarm. To make someone amused is to make them lose their mind. The word amusement is a compound word with the base word "muse", which means the mind. The prefix "a" means to take away. The suffix "ment" means "act or process". So the word amusement really means "the act or process of making one lose their mind." The predator's tactic in this situation is to keep his prey amused until he senses the other women are about to return. Then he springs for her number so that she will have to make a quick decision. Since he has disarmed her with charm and amused or made her lose her mind, she will give it to him without thinking. She may also do it consciously, if he is somewhat attractive to show the other women that this

Relationships

handsome man was interested in her. If she is smart, though, she will give him the pizza delivery number not her real number.

As you can see, a woman must be vigilant when she is out in public. She can never go where the adversary or his disciples can have an opportunity to attack her. She has to be especially vigilant if she has been in other abusive relationships. That is because her self-image and esteem have been damaged, which makes her vulnerable to other abusers. A predator can tell (almost smell) when a woman is vulnerable to abuse. His goal is to find a woman whom he believes has already suffered from abuse because she has more than likely already been conditioned to take abuse. If her father abused her mother, she will be attracted to some of the qualities of an abuser that made her love her father.

Ladies, this is one reason why some of your friends seem to go through one abusive relationship after another. Predatory men have perfected the art of identifying women who have been abused or are vulnerable to being abused. Thus, a woman, especially one who had been abused or exposed to abuse previously, can never allow herself to be chosen or picked by a man. When a man tries to pick her up, he is really trying to pick her off. A woman has to learn to set a standard for the type of man that she wants. She must learn to choose him, not allow him to choose her, and she cannot have sex with him until she is married.

An attempt to lead her into sexual activity early is a warning sign.

Sexual activity is a critical tool in an abusive man's methods of capture and control. Get my book "Maximizing Fatherhood" (https://www.drwillenterprises.com/fatherhood and study the chapter 11 "Marriage and Sex" to understand how an abuser uses the chemical make up of his body to cause a woman to become addicted to him and, thus, make it difficult for her to leave him. In nearly 30 years of observing domestic abuse cases, I have never seen a woman that was being abused by a man whom she was not having sex with.

MEN: SEX OUT OF WEDLOCK IS A FORM OF ABUSE

Ladies, you might as well turn to the next chapter because I am only speaking to the men here. There will be women who might get very angry at what I am going to say but I am not talking to them anyway. So save yourself the headache and turn the page.

When a man has sex with a woman who is not his wife, he is engaged in a form of abuse. Abuse is "abnormal use". Sex out of wedlock is the abnormal use of a woman because GOD did not intend for a woman to be used to gratify men's sexual desires and discarded. No matter how nice you are about it, going to bed with a woman who is

Relationships

not your wife is a form of sexual abuse! Since GOD made men to lead, we are held responsible for guiding a woman who may be offering herself to us in the right way.

Most men were never taught how to respond to a woman in the right way. Therefore, we fail in our responsibility to respond appropriately especially since the broader society does not seem to frown on unwedded sexual activity. But just because a woman offers herself to us it does not mean that we have to accept. We seem to have no problem turning away the so-called "ugly" woman. Yet, we act like we do not have the ability to do the same with one that is pretty, hot, and tempting. We all know that at the end of the day we are going to walk away from the woman who appears to be "too easy". The average man wants to marry a woman who we believe to be virtuous. No matter how good or hot a woman looks none of us would have sex with her if we knew she has AIDS. Therefore, we could and would abstain from having sex out of wedlock if we understood our responsibility before GOD and learned to be responsible, become response able, or obtained response ability in order to consistently respond to women appropriately.

GOD put 43 different hormones in a man's body that is designed to make women attracted and responsive to men sexually. These hormones were created to make men and women bond to one another. Over a period of time the two of them engaging in sex regularly causes them to become physically, spiritually and emotionally bonded chemically. This is the reason why it hurts and makes the average woman crazy when we just leave her or walk away. These hormones give a man an advantage and a certain amount of power over women. When we misuse the power that GOD gave us by taking advantage of a woman who is merely responding to us the way GOD designed her that is a form of abuse.

The reason it is becoming more and more critical for men to maintain control sexually is because the media has been subtly programming our minds to accept the notion that sex out of wedlock is ok. (There is a reason why TV shows are called programs.) But sexual activity with multiple partners is devastating over time to a woman's emotional wellbeing. Then, when a man sees a woman who looks whole and beautiful and decides to marry her, he suddenly realizes that she has been exposed to a type of abuse and has been affected mentally and emotionally.

Therefore, we men have to understand that leading a woman into sex out of wedlock is a form of abuse. It is an abnormal use of the woman for our personal gratification and it is an abuse of the power that GOD placed in us. We must recognize that it contributes to making women (as men say) crazy, and take responsibility for ending sex without commitment by marrying the woman who we would love to make love to.

Relationships

the outward appearance, look at what he has in his heart." This is what a woman must also do, particularly in today's society. A man may be tall, handsome, and have the look of a king and a warrior, but he may be a coward at heart. He may have a nice physique, a nice car, clothes, and jewelry but he could actually be broke. This is why it is wise for a woman to not only examine a man's assets, but also to learn who he really is, the assets of his character and qualities before she invests in him physically and emotionally. Then, she will learn whether he would be a good husband before she gives him the benefits that should be reserved for her husband.

We cannot judge a tree by its leaves. Dead trees will continue to grow leaves but they will not produce fruit. You will know a tree by the fruit it produces. We try to judge people by their leaves, i.e. their house, car, clothes, jewelry, or income. However, we must learn to judge them by the fruit they produce or it will continue to lead us into stressful relationships. If the produce of their life is not the fruit of the spirit which is love, joy, peace, patience, and temperance, they are actually spiritually dead.

The fruit that spiritually dead people produce is adultery, fornication, impurity, idolatry, lasciviousness, witchcraft, opposition, debate, jealousy, wrath, strife, division, disunion, envying, murdering, drunkenness, and other like things. When you are looking for someone to love and marry, they must have the spirit of GOD in them

Relationships

or they will not be able to truly love you. They may have an intense like or lust for you, but like and lust are not fruits of the spirit so they cannot grow into love. Everything reproduces after its own kind. Lust is a perversion of love so lust can only grow into other perversions. The lust that a person has for you will lead them into contention with you and into lust with others. If fornication, for example, was the foundation of a relationship, it will produce adultery in your marriage. This is why the old saying is true "If they did it with you they will do it to you."

Since GOD instructed the Prophet not look at the outward man when trying to identify a man's qualities and characteristics, we should operate under that guidance as well. When a man approaches you who appears to be good, a woman's job is to get him to talk. You can never know what is in a man's heart (the heart of his mind) unless you listen to what comes out of his mouth. Jesus said "Out of the abundance of the heart, the mouth speaks." Get him to explain to you in detail who he is, where he is going, what his vision is, and how he plans to lead a family and raise his children. Get him to explain it again to you at different times and on different occasions. Listen to be sure his answers are consistent.

The reason you have to do this is because any man can figure out what you want to hear over time by what you say. Any man can come up with something that sounds good. The world is full of "one day I'm gonna brothers".

If a man is serious about doing anything, he will have already done something to further his plans. So don't say much and just let him talk. Make sure his answers sound like what he should say based on what you have read in this book. Make sure also that the he answers he gives are consistent. Then, you will know that the knowledge coming out of his mouth is in his heart and not just something popping off the top of his head.

Along with the qualities of a king and warrior, a good man will have the characteristics of a mentor and a friend. The man who is a mentor will be a teacher as well as a preacher and acts as a life developer, guide, or coach for others. He uses his life to teach others the ways of righteousness and encourages them to do what's right because it's right. He is a spiritual cheerleader who leads by example with his life rather than his lips. A friend is a peacemaker. He is emotionally connected to others and sensitive to their needs. He is unselfish, always available to give grace to help in the time of need, and ever ready to give wise counsel.

A man with the qualities and characteristics of a king, warrior, mentor and friend is faithful man. A faithful man walks in the integrity of his heart. His wife and children will be blessed after him as a result. He is a man with uprightness of character and unquestionable honesty. A faithful man is sober and sound in spirit, mind, and body. He is complete, not looking for external fulfillment or instant gratification, and does not have a need to seduce other women. A faithful man is stable, consistent over time, and not found lacking when tested for excellence.

THE ESSENTIAL ELEMENTS OF MANHOOD

In addition to being able to identify the faithful man, having a set of standards that women can use to identify a "real" man will help reduce a need for the 911 type of emergency assistance in many relationships. A lot of arguments and physical fights start or escalate when women say to men "be a man" or "be a real man". This statement drives men crazy because they don't really know what women mean. Most women don't seem to be in agreement as to what a "man" or "real man" is. Different women have different ideas of what a man or real man is and that definition sometimes changes depending on which show they watched, magazine they read, or radio program they listened to that day.

Having knowledge on the essential elements that go into making a male a man will help women identify a "real" man when they see him and hopefully keep them from getting sexually involved with a big boy who is not a real man. Perhaps knowing this will stop women from discarding and dismissing a faithful man when he shows up because they perceived him to be just another man sized boy. Understanding the essential elements of manhood will also provide men with knowledge to reinforce in themselves and teach their sons what a man should essentially be.

The phrase "essential element" means a thing cannot be what it is supposed to be if it is missing this thing or things. The essential elements of a cake, for example, are flour and sugar. Without sugar a cake is just bread. Without flour the rest of those elements baked together just make a mess. In order for an adult male to be a man there are 15 essential elements that he must retain in his inner being that becomes a part of who he is as an individual. These elements, ladies, are essential to a man having the maturity and responsibility to properly lead a family. If you don't see them in the man you are considering marrying, then you will know that you are not about to marry a man. He may be a full grown adult male in stature but he is still a boy in essence.

Essential element of manhood #1: Integrity. Integrity is a state of complete mental, emotional, intellectual, moral and ethical development where a man becomes mature or single. That is, whole within himself and connected and one with GOD. Integrity is proven when these attributes are tested and a man is found to remain strong in his commitment to GOD, his wife, and his family. A man retains his integrity at all costs because he understands that integrity is more easily kept than recovered.

Relationships

You will know if a man has integrity once his character or the distinctive qualities of his personality or nature are tested. A person with integrity is actually who he appears to be. Like Popeye ("I am what I am") a man with integrity is not pretentious. You will find him to have a consistency of personality and character. When he is under pressure, you will find him steadfast and unmovable.

Imagine someone with their fingers interlaced. Then imagine two people standing on each side of that person trying to pull their fingers apart. A man with integrity is strong and mentally tough enough to keep his fingers interlaced. This is an illustration of what will happen if a woman comes along and tries to pull him away from his wife on one side and satan tries to pull him away from GOD on the other side. The strength of his character makes him tough enough to keep his fingers interlaced or to remain connected with GOD and one with his wife under an extreme amount of pressure. By the strength of his character a man can get a woman to marry him, but without integrity he can't keep her from divorcing him.

Essential element of manhood #2: Excellence. A man with excellence transcends other men in quality, merit or skill. He is highly sought after and nearly without peer in business and industry because no one can do what he does quite the way he does it or as well as he does it. He breeds this quality into his family. His children become eminently good, powerful and productive as a result of his example and influence.

Each person was created to be unique like a snowflake. There is no one who has your DNA, finger print, retinal pattern, palm print, foot print, etc. There is no one with your unique set of knowledge, gifts, talents, and abilities that was given by GOD to fulfill your unique purpose. We were ALL born, built and bred for excellence. Men who are excellent simply step up or grow into what they were originally created by GOD to be.

Sadly, however, men and boys have difficulty reaching this level of quality these days because we are trained and conditioned through the education system and society to be mediocre. 70% is enough to pass to the next grade level and we advance without being pushed to excellence; or pushed to achieve greatness. Most of us succumb to the pressure of our peers to not appear very smart because nobody likes anybody who knows everything.

Men of excellence are internally driven to exceed well beyond mediocrity and have learned to advance to a high level where they don't have many peers. They take the hard jobs that no one else wants and do the job better than anybody who has ever done it before. Men of excellence do what is right because it is right and they do it right the first time.

Relationships

Essential elements of manhood #3: Bravery. Every a man must have intestinal fortitude or the courage to stand in the face of adversity and drive on. Being brave is not being without fear. Bravery is having the capacity to defend one's self or family in spite of fear. There is a difference between bravery and bravado or swagger. Many young people today think that having swagger or "swag" is cool. However, according to the dictionary, swagger is just a superficial show of confidence. A real man does not have swagger but rather he has the real quality of bravery. A man must possess the bravery to tenaciously defend his wife and family. He must have the quality of bravery internally in order to teach his sons to be brave because a chump can't raise a champ.

Now, bravery is a very important element of manhood because physical security is a primary need for a woman. She has to know that her man can defend her and keep her safe physically or she will begin looking for a man who has the quality of bravery. "Fontes fortuna juvat" – fortune favors the brave.

Essential element of manhood #4: Knowledgeable. Knowledge is science. In order for a man to effectively serve a family he must have a grasp of knowledge in five sciences: Religion, law, medicine, politics, and history. If his family has a problem the solution is going to more than likely reside in one of those areas. A man does not need to be an expert in any of them but he does need some knowledge of all of them.

Grown men become prideful when they have a lack of knowledge. Pride is a defense mechanism that can arise once a man sees in a woman's eyes that she know that he lacks knowledge about how to be a man, husband, father, and leader. When women begin to pressure prideful men to be what they are supposed to be and to operate in what they are supposed to know ("Be a man!"), it is like throwing a match on gas. A prideful man is puffed up, full of hot air, and is combustible. A man who is full of pride can't take the heat so he explodes. A lack of knowledge is what often ignites domestic violence.

Prideful men can't allow themselves to be reduced in the eyes of the woman in lives so they will try to use their physical strength against the woman to relieve the pressure and "prove"they are a man. Once you recognize that a man lacks knowledge and is full of pride it means that he is potentially a striker. It is best, therefore, not to argue or fight with him. He is best just left alone.

Essential element of manhood #5: Prudent. A prudent man is intelligent, successful, and understanding. He is a wise guide in the management of a family's affairs and sees no value in having an extramarital affair. He has learned to circumscribe his desires and keep his passions within due bounds. His passion and desire is reserved and released for activities with his wife. He is a proper example for his children.

Relationships

Essential element of manhood #6: Patient. A patient man is able to bear the trials and tribulations of life calmly and without much complaint. He has the discipline to not retaliate immediately when provoked and understands that reacting emotionally is a luxury afforded to women and children. He has the intestinal fortitude to remain steadfast despite opposition, difficulties or adversities.

The majority of men who are locked up in the penitentiary for violent crimes committed an act as an emotional response to something someone else had done or they are there as a result of making a hasty decision. Rashness is the parent of misfortune. I have never seen a man fall into misfortune that was not preceded by a hasty act or where he made a decision without due caution. Men who react emotionally or hastily are dangerous because of the power to hurt or maim that they hold in their hands. Therefore, men must be deliberative rather than emotional in their response to any situation. This is why patience is a virtue. It is also why the virtuous woman and the faithful man are a perfect match.

Essential element of manhood #7: Faithful. Faithful in this context is not a reference to sexual fidelity; it is merely a byproduct of it. A faithful man is reliable, trustworthy, established, stable, consistent, and dependable. He is a guardian of his wife's virtue and has the ability to nurture and care for his children. Men who don't have a faithful quality are not ready to lead and care for a wife and family.

"Most men will proclaim everyone his own goodness: but a faithful man who can find (Proverbs 20:6)." "Who can find a virtuous woman? For her price is far above rubies (Proverbs 31:10)."

The perfect man for a virtuous woman is a faithful man. The effort to keep a virtuous woman, one with strength power and moral excellence, from a faithful man is the reason why the adversary wages a persistent attack against women using men. The union of a faithful man and virtuous woman is too powerful for the devil or his demons to deal with and are a threat to his very existence. Therefore, he works to harden women's hearts against men using deceived men so that when the faithful man comes along they will reject him. "He's too nice!"

Faithful men see their families as the beginning and the end of their existence. Faithful in family is the reason, in their hearts, why GOD placed them here. Faithful men also recognize that the only hands GOD has in the earth are the ones attached to the end of our arms. The only power Jesus has in the earth to fulfill His mission is through His bride; she has to put Him on (Galatians 3:27) so that He can have the power to do what He needs to do.

Similarly, a faithful man needs a virtuous woman to put him on like a jacket. The mission or purpose of a jacket

Relationships

is to cover and protect but it cannot do what it was designed or created to do unless someone puts it on. Once someone puts it on, it receives the power it needs to do what it was designed to do. Once a virtuous woman "puts on" a faithful man, he obtains the power and strength to complete his mission or purpose as well as to cover and protect her.

Essential element of manhood #8: Loyal. A loyal man is unswerving in allegiance to his wife and family but his first obligation is to GOD. Loyalty is a quality that makes a man want to sacrifice his life to save the lives of his loved ones. His sons learn loyalty by him making it their duty to protect their mother and sisters. Loyal men are law abiding and work hard to get ahead rather than devise schemes to get over.

Loyalty is the character quality the scripture is urging us to grow into that said "Submitting yourselves one to another in the fear of GOD." Husbands and wives must be loyal to our spouses but we owe our first loyalty to GOD. As we follow HIS guidance to submit ourselves one to another; to get under, support, or help our spouses to complete or fulfill the mission they were assigned to do, we must NOT do anything that GOD would not want us to do. If we are struggling to pay bills or we don't have the money needed to fulfill our mission, for example, we cannot allow our spouse to convince us to help them rob a bank.

Some men accuse their wife of not having their back or lacking loyalty when they refuse to support them in a mission that is wrong, unethical or criminal. He tries to make her feel guilty when he is the one who actually lacks loyalty. A man that is loyal to his wife would not ask her to do something he knows she does not want to do. It is a statement that he doesn't care if she has to go to jail or will feel badly once she does help him. He simply wants to do what he wants to do. And he appears to have a need to drag someone else into disloyalty before GOD with him. A man who is loyal will always do what is right for his wife regardless of what she might want him to do.

Essential element of manhood #9: Honest. An honest man is believable and truthful when tested over time. He has an unwavering quality of being a decent, fitting and proper husband. An honest man strenuously protects the reputation of his name. He knows that he only owns two things in life: his word and his name. Everything else that he owns can be taken away but he can only lose his good name by not keeping his word. Honesty is the character quality that determines a man's credibility (credit ability) or whether or not he is credit worthy. If a man has good credit it is a good indication that he is fairly honest.

Essential element of manhood #10: Selfless. A selfless man is one who believes it's important to place the needs of others come before his own. This quality drives some women crazy because they can't argue with him. In every case where it doesn't make a difference he is going to let her have her way. It may make him seem weak to her when he won't fight for what he wants but what he wants is for her to have what she wants.

Selflessness can appear to be weakness to some women until they understand that selflessness is a type of strength. Selflessness is what the Bible calls "meekness" which means to have one's "power under control". Jesus could have called down 10,000 angels to help him down from the cross but because he was meek he kept his power under control in order to complete his mission and please His Father. A meek or selfless man's main desire is to please those he loves in his quest to maintain peace and harmony within his family.

"...the meek shall inherit the earth; and shall delight themselves in the abundance of peace (Psalm 37:11)."

Selfless is also synonymous with egoless. Our ultimate mission in life as men is to become egoless and to awaken to the reality to who GOD created us to be. That is, to be reborn out of our current selfish, self centered, or prideful ego state into an egoless state where we become conscious to who we really are. In order for a man to actually be "born again" he must first become selfless. Then he can truly experience life and love in peace.

Essential element of manhood #11: Responsible. Responsible men are accountable and answerable to their wives. They are able to hold the duty, trust and position of husband and father. Responsible men understand they must be able to respond to the needs of their wife and family. Thus when it is time for them to respond they have the ability to respond appropriately. A man who has the ability to respond, then, is response able.

Growing up in a home under the nurture and guidance of a mother and having a job when a boy is young is simply the training he needs to be able to handle the responsibilities he will have as a man. A boy learns to be accountable to his mother so that he will have no problem being answerable to his wife. He learns to perform his duty and retain trust in his position on a job so that he will know how to execute his duty and retain trust in his position as husband and father. A man can never be given the responsibility of a wife and family unless he has demonstrated that he has the ability to respond to them properly.

Learning to submit to the authority of his father gives a boy the discipline he needs to be, not just an adult male but, a real man. The best place for a boy to learn discipline is in the home from his father. However, there are only two places where a boy can learn discipline (besides the military): either the play pen or the state pen. If he does not learn discipline from his father at home, he will be forced to learn it from men in jail. Learning discipline teaches a boy to be responsible. Giving a boy duty and responsibility will keep him out of the penitentiary.

Essential element of manhood #12: Good. A good man has a positive moral quality that is beneficial to his family. The quality of his good character makes him a strong powerful leader. Others follow him because they want to not because they have to. He is the epitome of a winner. He is a courageous intelligent decision maker, is often well spoken of, highly regarded, and a man who can make his family woman wealthy.

A good man understands that a candle does not lose anything when it lights another candle; it only spreads more light. Thus he is eager to help his family become the best they can be. A good man also the type of man who:

1. Conforms to the moral order of the universe
2. Has a praiseworthy character
3. Advances prosperity or well being
4. Is useful or beneficial to others
5. Has economic utility or satisfies an economic desire
6. Has the qualities to achieve an end
7. Is an example by which bad men are revealed to women

Essential element of manhood #13: Kind. A kind man is benevolent, eager to serve and gracious to his wife and family. He is observed by others to be giving, easy to get along with, and has a loving manner. Kind men have a natural state of being where it's easy to see that being kind is not what they do, it's who they are. The one thing kind men hate, however, is when people mistake their kindness for weakness.

A man who is kind has the ability to easily influence others as they see no danger in opening themselves up to him. Influence means to breathe into or inspire. It is similar to influenza which is caused by someone breathing on you and causing the infection they have in them begin to grow in you. When a person influences, inspires or breathes into you, a part of them or some of what is contained in their spirit goes into and becomes a part of your spirit. Their influence begins to affect how you think, effect what you do, and infect your life. Men who are kind have the capacity to inspire and therefore to affect, effect and infect their wife and children which helps him lead them to achieve their family's mission or goals.

People don't care how much you know until they know how much you care (Dr Cornell West "borrowed" this maxim from me).Thus kind men are excellent teachers who have the ability to lead their family to do extraordinary things.

Relationships

Essential element of manhood #14: Love. A man with the quality of love lives his life and loves his wife with passion, devotion and tenderness. His love is expressed through freedom, justice and equality. A flower must willingly give up its life to allow us to express our love. A man who not only has love but IS love will be willing to die to his own life in order to express his love to his wife and children.

The secret to success in life is to stay in love! Love gives us the fire needed to ignite other people, the insight to recognize the good qualities in them, and a passionate desire to do things for them. A person who is not in love doesn't have the kind of excitement that helps propel them ahead. The quickest way to get ahead is to help others achieve. You can have everything you want in life as long as you help as many people as you can get what they need. It takes love to make that kind of sacrifice. There is nothing more powerful, motivating and exhilarating in life than love.

Essential element of manhood #15: Blessed. Every man who is blessed was empowered by GOD to prosper. He has inherent knowledge, gifts, talents, and abilities that when marketed properly someone will pay him for handsomely. Blessed men understand when GOD said HE gave them the power to get wealth that GOD was actually talking about his wife. A single man can become rich but a man with the right wife can become wealthy.

In order to be blessed or endowed with the power to prosper, a man has to complete the process of alchemy. Alchemy is said to be a process of turning lead into gold however it is actually the transformation our lower self into our higher self. Alchemy changes a man from something virtually useless into something highly valuable. He sheds that selfish, cheating, stealing, lying, etc., character quality and puts on a new prudent, patient, faithful, loyal, honest, selfless, etc., identity. A man who was once just a lead weight in the world then becomes a valuable commodity to the world, his wife, and family.

In His famous "Sermon on the Mount" Jesus recites a number of character traits commonly known as the "beatitudes" that are held by those who are blessed or have completed the alchemical process. This list is actually a series of attitudes that a man must "be" in mind, body and spirit in order to be blessed or empowered to prosper. Jesus said blessed are those who "BE":

a. Poor in spirit – this is the opposite of greedy or selfish. A person who is poor in spirit gives freely and does not worry about hoarding or putting things away for rainy days because he has faith that GOD will always provide.

Relationships

b. Mournful – to have empathy or compassion for others; is apt to teach to give others knowledge needed toovercome their state or condition. Mournful people are effective teachers because they teach out of love.

c. Thirsty for righteousness – or to be in right standing with GOD. They want to do what is right because it isright.

d. Merciful – is not quick to punish or condemn others for their faults, mistakes, or misjudgments.

e. Pure in heart – are those who have a natural abundance of love and affection for all people

f. Peacemaker – reconcile disputes between others or helps to lead people back into the grace of GOD.

When you cannot find men as they ought to be you won't find women as they ought to be. Women are always affected by men. It seems reasonable to conclude then that if you find a wise man, you should be able to find one wise woman. However, in a corrupt environment a wise man is too well ordered, too good to be true, and is rejected by the very women who are seeking a good man.

The reason the Bible is written in patriarchal position is not because men are superior to women, it's because GOD knew that if men were in order the women and children would be alright. A well ordered man comes fully equipped with all of the essential elements of manhood. The problem in modern times is a woman cannot see anything in a well ordered man's life that he would "need" her for. Besides being made suspicious by the world, society and church that nobody can be perfect, this is one of the reasons a good woman rejects the well ordered man. She chooses instead the unordered, undisciplined or unrighteous man because she can see where she can help "fix" him to become what she needs him to be. But ultimately she only becomes as he is.

In order for a woman to become the best woman she can be, her husband has to already be the best man that he can be before they get married. The best man for a woman will have all 15 of the essential elements of manhood.

WHY ARE THERE 15 ESSENTIAL ELEMENTS OF MANHOOD?

I don't really want to add this section because it is a little heady and it exposes my inner nerd. However, I feel compelled to include it because I always get the question: Why are their 15 essential elements of manhood? So I will try to explain it as briefly as I can. If you are not really interested in the answer to the question, you may want to go on to the next section.

Relationships

Man was made by GOD to operate in the same way as the earth and universe.

He was organized by GOD to be in harmony with his environment in order to be an effective ruler over and keeper of it. Everything in the earth and universe is currently moving from duality to unity; from being separate to becoming one. The reason we can see further and further out into space is not just because of the Hubble Telescope but because the universe is getting smaller. Consequently, everything that pertains to mankind must also move from duality to unity.

When we see a number that has dual elements, like 15, we must move that number into its unifying factor or force which in this case is 6 (1+5=6). All of the numbers that appear in the Bible have a meaning. The number 6 represents the number of man in that man was created on the 6th day. The 6th verse in every chapter of Genesis, the book of creation, is a reference to mankind, a man, or men. If a man's mother was standing up when he was born, he would come into the world upside down or with his head pointing toward the ground, emblematic of the number 6.

An adult male must have 15 qualities that form the totality of his character in order to be organized into a whole or complete man. That is, a man who is in union or harmony with himself, the earth and the universe. The union of 1 and 5 make 6, which is the bible number of man. The combination of all 15 essential qualities in unity makes a man whole, complete, or perfect.

The essential elements of manhood are actually the 15 character qualities of Jesus Christ. An adult male must have all of these qualities to create a harmonious home environment and to be an effective leader for his family. Having all of these qualities prepares him to be the "perfect" man, husband, and father.

Now, this is the point where we depart from the wisdom of the world, society, and even traditional church teaching because we are instructed by all three that "nobody's perfect", "no one CAN be perfect", "the only one who was perfect was Jesus", etc. However, consider the reason why GOD said that HE gave man the five-fold ministry in Ephesians 4:11 (4+11=15).

"And he gave some apostles, and some prophets; and some evangelists; and some pastors and teachers: for the PERFECTING of the saints, for the work of the ministry, for the edifying of the body of Christ: Till we all come in the UNITY of the faith and of the knowledge of the Son of GOD unto a PERFECT man, unto the measure of the stature of the fullness of Christ…"

It is stated twice here that the main reason for the 5 fold ministry is to make a man perfect. However, in an effort to make the world's wisdom conform to the word of GOD, we are told that the word "perfect" here means mature. If you check any definition of any form of the word perfect in any Greek or Hebrew lexicon you will NOT find the word "mature" in any of them. The closest you will come to the word mature is the definition that contains the phrase "of full age". But, even that phrase is NOT referring to a person being mature. Rather it is a reference to the completion or fulfillment of one's responsibility before GOD in the "age" or time in which they live. This is what is commonly referred to as "purpose". When a man has completed or fulfilled his GOD ordained purpose in the time period which he lived, he comes into "full age" or perfect before GOD with regard to his duty. He becomes a son like Jesus in whom GOD is well pleased. This is the only way that a man can hear GOD say "Well done thy faithful servant, enter ye into the joy of the Lord (Matthew 25).

In order to become "perfect" in his humanity, a man must become as Jesus is. We are taught that this is impossible but, again, this is one of the reasons why GOD gave us the five-fold ministry: to teach us to measure up to Jesus in mental, physical and spiritual stature. "Let this mind be in you which was also in Christ Jesus who being in the form of GOD thought it not robbery to be equal with GOD (Philippians 2:5)." Once we "let" ourselves think like Jesus does we can become as Jesus is.

Notice the last clause of the Ephesians 4 verse above "...unto the measure of the stature of the fullness of Christ...". That means, when the world tries to examine or measure our lives in comparison to Jesus, they should not be able to tell the difference between us and Him. The only way the world can see Christ is through Christians. So, if they were to see us standing next to Jesus they should not be able to tell the difference. A man must reach the measure of the stature of Jesus in order to be well pleasing to GOD and it should not take him most of his lifetime. The growth that a man must go through in this regard is represented by the numbers on the face of a clock.

The number 12 is the seat of GOD; it represents "eternal perfection" in the union of the trinity $1+2=3$. We were created in heaven or the spirit realm and resided with GOD before we were born into the earth. We move metaphorically across the face of the clock once we depart the spiritual realm of heaven with each number representing a stage of growth until we ultimately get back to the 12 or return to GOD. Hopefully, we will return to HIM triumphantly or in glory having completed or fulfilled the purpose for which we were sent into the earth.

The number 1 means "union", 2 means "unity, and 3 means "divinity". We are still in divine union with GOD while in the first trimester of development in our mother's womb. The number 4 means "the world" which is the beginning of the second trimester, or the 4th month. That is when most mothers began to "show" that our presence in the world is imminent. The number 5 means "grace" or power. As we are in our final stages of development we are endued with power while we are yet unborn. This is how John the Baptist was able to recognize Jesus in Mary's womb while John was only a 6 month old fetus (Luke 1:36-41). We are born at the number 6, upside down, and our primary goal at this point is to turn our lives right side up, get our head to the sky, orient our way of thinking toward GOD, or become upright in stature.

We need the 5 fold ministry to provide the knowledge we need to empower us to turn toward GOD and become complete. That is, whole within ourselves and connected and one with GOD. The number 7 means "completion". Once we become complete within ourselves we are ready to begin a new life. The number 8 means "new beginning". This is the point where we are positioned to move up to the next level and obtain victory over our lives by turning 180° (1+8=9) within ourselves. We turn from being upside down in our mind, body and spirit morally and spiritually to being right-side up or in line with heaven. If we don't get beyond the number 8 level of development, we will be condemned to renewing ourselves daily. Every time we sin we will have to start over and over and over again. This is why the symbol for infinity is the number 8 turned on its side. Rather than being 180° out of phase with GOD at the position 6 level of growth, we remain stuck at the 240° mark in our growth and transition back to GOD (2+4=6). While we may have progressed into adulthood physically, morally and spiritually we remain stuck at a child-like level of development equivalent to the level 6. The overwhelming majority of people who attend church every week are stuck in this position. Yet, neither they nor their pastors can figure out why they go to church every week, some several times per week, but they never grow. They become "born again" or reach the level 8 or new beginning level of development and get stuck in that position; physical adults but moral and spiritual babies (Hebrews 5:12-14).

The number 9 means "victory" which represents the victory that we obtain over ourselves. The propensity that we have to sin that once lived within ourselves has been overcome. Our head and heart is now constantly pointed in the direction of GOD. Once we overcome ourselves, we must now learn to overcome the world. This process is symbolically represented by the number 10. After we have overcome ourselves and the world, the 0 part of our personality (that is retained by influence from the world) is added to the 1 and thereby canceled out. This now makes us 1 or whole in mind, body and spirit. We no longer have 2 personalities (1 and 0; good and no good). We are no longer double minded as a result of being complete in Christ but influenced by the world. We are totally 1 now within ourselves and connected and one with GOD once

Relationships

we complete the process of overcoming the world.

This process is how we grow from duality and conflict in mind, body, and spirit into unity of mind, body, and spirit. Now we should understand what "forsake not the assembly of ourselves together" is actually instructing us to do in Hebrews 10:25. The context of the 10th chapter of Hebrews 10 pertains to overcoming sin. The 25th verse of that chapter is not instructing us to go to church as we are taught. We must assemble our mind, body and spirit together within ourselves so that they become "single" or 1 in order to become whole within ourselves and connected and one with GOD. If we do not assemble our mind, body, and spirit in unity, we will not be able to break free from the root of sin that is living within us.

Sin creates conflict between the mind, body, and spirit over whether to remain connected to the world or to become connected and one with GOD. That is why the average person that goes to church regularly, says they are born again, and says that they love GOD vacillates frequently between living right and doing wrong. Once we break free through assembling ourselves within, we will be recognized as a child of the Host High GOD (1 John 3:2-10). Once we see Jesus we will know Him because we shall be like Him. Then, as we stand next to the #1 Son of GOD, the world won't be able to tell the difference between us and Him.

This is what the number 11 on the clock face represents; you or me who have become 1 or single and standing next to Jesus. Heretofore, we were only spiritually positioned in oneness with GOD. At this point we are positioned to become physically connected with GOD. "No man comes to the Father but by me." We have to become as Jesus IS if we hope to return to GOD or back to the number 12 which is in union or eternal perfection with GOD.

Sadly, few of us ever make it to become as Jesus is because we are told that we can't. Few men ever attain the 15 essential elements of manhood because we are led to believe it is impossible for a man to have all of these qualities; to be perfect. Whenever a man does not know he is supposed to obtain something he rarely does. Consequently, women have no knowledge on what a man is supposed to be before they get married. They end up with a man who does not have all that he needs to know or possess in order to be a perfect husband and father. Women learn to tolerate men for as long as they can and some just ultimately divorce him. The man did the best he could but nobody ever told him what he was supposed to know. Nobody told him that he was supposed to develop the character and qualities of Jesus before he got married.

Although Peter did actually walk on water, most men are told that no man walked on water but Jesus (Matthew 14:28-29). We are given the false illusion that nobody could be as Jesus IS when this is the main reason why

Relationships

GOD gave us the 5 fold ministry. Its purpose is to empower us to be as Jesus is. The primary reason why we must become like Jesus is to convict the world to come to Christ. In order to obtain a conviction in a court of law you must have substantial evidence. In order to convict a person to come to Christ we must have substantial evidence that He IS and that He is indeed the Son of GOD. The world would rather see a sermon than hear one any day. The only way the world can see evidence that Jesus IS, is through us. People of the world should obtain the hope that they too can become as Jesus is by seeing that we are like Him.

Now, there are sciences that we can apply to verify this information but I do not want to make what may already be confusing to some more complicated. Just know, however, that the Theory of Relativity ($e=mc^2$), the Pythagorean Theorem ($a^2+b^2=c^2$), and quantum physics will help us understand how a man can become as Jesus is before he reaches 20 years of age. It is actually supposed to happen by the time he is 12 or 13 but certainly by the time he is 14. This is why the Orthodox Jews celebrate their sons reaching manhood at this age with a bar mitzvah. In Africa and other parts of the world a boy's transition into manhood is celebrated at this age with a rite of passage. A boy should be taught or trained to obtain the essential qualities of manhood; to become a perfect man, husband, and father before he reaches the age of manhood.

A boy needs both a mother and father to learn to obtain the essential elements of manhood. You see, some of those elements have a feminine quality and character. This is one reason why GOD would not allow Mary to raise Jesus as a single mother. Joseph had decided to leave her because he knew the baby wasn't his but GOD made him go back and raise that boy. Again, a boy learns these essential qualities from both parents (those parents who know they are supposed to be taught) but he learns integrity, excellence, knowledge, bravery, prudence, patience and faithfulness primarily from his father and he learns to be, loyal, honest, selfless, responsible, good, kind, love and blessed primarily from his mother. Without these essential qualities a man will struggle to be the best man that he can be for his wife and family.

FATHER VS DADDY

The way we use the word "father" is faulty which prevents us from identifying between the faithful man and the fool. The men who provided the seed for the child often get credit for being a father on days like Father's Day when they never even raised or took care of a child. The word "father" is used in our society to describe a man who guides, guards, and governs; directs, corrects and protects as well as provides and cares for a child. However, that definition more accurately describes a Dad.

Relationships

A father is actually one who provides the seed for birth. It does not matter whether he raises that child or not, he becomes a "father" once he provides the seed for the child. A Dad, on the other hand, is a man who loves and provides the mental, physical, emotional, and financial support for the child. A dad is the man who is always there with and for that child till the end through thick and thin. It does not matter to a "real" dad whether or not he provided the seed that fathered the child. A dad is going to love the child as if it came from his seed anyway. Any male can be a father but only a real man can be a dad! Every father is not a dad. And some dads have never actually fathered a child. But they love the children whom they raise and are a daddy to as if they were of their own blood.

Fathers do not direct a child into destiny because they are not raising the child. It is daddy that determines destiny. Men who fathered children that are not raising them do so because they have not learned how to arrive at or walk into their destiny. This occurs primarily because they didn't have a daddy.

Everything in life is comprised of a trinity. There are 3 parts from the smallest particle of life or the atom (electron, proton, and neutron) to the human being (spirit, soul, body) the essence of everything comes down to 3 primary parts. Each person has three single digit numbers assigned to their life when they are born. These numbers are, 1 through 9, which represent a complete entity in life and its purpose for being. The three represent our identity, personality, and destiny. The destiny number is commonly referred to as the life number but it is not. The life number is a fourth number that changes depending on where we are in life on our journey to spiritual growth. There is a book entitled "The Wisdom of the Enneagram: The Complete Guide To Spiritual Growth For The Nine Personality Types", Don Richard Riso and Russ Hudson, that can shed greater light on this subject.

I am not going to go into this too deeply because there are religious people who will try to convince you that this science is something evil. Historically, people have labeled things as evil in an effort to distract us from the truth and to lead us away from the knowledge we need to find and fulfill our earthly assignment. The destiny number along with the knowledge, gifts, talents, and abilities that we were born with inherently provide clues to help us discover the assignment we were given life to complete.

Crucial to the child achieving their destiny is the father achieving victory over himself. That is, he must reach the spiritual development level of the 9. When a child's identity, personality, and destiny numbers are added to the father's life number that is a 9, the child can come to know who they are, how they are supposed to behave, and what they were assigned by GOD to do. If the father

Relationships

has become a regenerated man, or a 9, the child will be able to become whatever he or she was created to become. However, if the father tries to add his life to the child's life while he is still an unregenerate man, or a 6, the child will never come to be what he or she was meant to become. Whatever the child turns out to be will be impacted by how far the father was able to travel on the path of righteousness. This is because any number you add to 9 will come to be itself.

Take a look at the following illustration. Anything that 9 is added to will return unto itself.

$$1 + 9 = 10 = 1 \quad 5 + 9 = 14 = 5 \quad 9 + 9 = 18 = 9$$
$$2 + 9 = 11 = 2 \quad 6 + 9 = 15 = 6 \quad 10 + 9 = 19 = 10$$
$$3 + 9 = 12 = 3 \quad 7 + 9 = 16 = 7$$
$$4 + 9 = 13 = 4 \quad 8 + 9 = 17 = 8$$

$$1 + 6 = 7 = 0 \quad 5 + 6 = 11 = 2 \quad 9 + 6 = 15 = 6$$
$$2 + 6 = 8 = 0 \quad 6 + 6 = 12 = 3 \quad 10 + 6 = 16 = 7$$
$$3 + 6 = 9 = 0 \quad 7 + 6 = 13 = 4$$
$$4 + 6 = 10 = 1 \quad 8 + 6 = 14 = 5$$

Fathers must achieve victory over themselves in order to lead their children to become victors. When we have not come to be whom GOD created us to be, it is impossible to lead our children to become who HE created them to be. We must already be what we expect our children to become. Parents who were not prepared for victory by their natural parents must make GOD their Father. In HIM is the victory that overcomes the world. Then, we can prepare our children for victory. When parents cover ourselves with victory, we can cover the children with our lives. This will prepare the children to leave home dressed to the 9s.

It is difficult for a child become what they were created to be if their daddy has not yet reached his full potential or capacity. Men who have a heart to be a daddy for a child help them to arrive at and walk into their destiny. We can solve one of the problems that cause rampant fatherlessness in American society by first teaching men how to arrive at and walk into their own destiny. Then, those men will have a heart to be a daddy and return to raise their children.

When it comes to solving problems, I believe in the "Tea Kettle Theory".If you have a problem with the noise a tea kettle is making, the optimum solution is not to plug up the hole in the top where the noise is coming from. The optimum solution is to turn the fire off at the bottom. Once you turn the fire off the noise will never be a problem again unless you turn the fire back on. Once we get to the bottom or the root cause of any issue, we can eliminate ALL of them. They will never come back unless we allow that which was the root cause to return.

Relationships

Now, there is a difference between solving a problem and helping a problem. Providing after school programs or midnight basketball for children who have been abandoned by their fathers is helping the problem. Providing food stamps and welfare helps the problem of children in poverty. That is, it only helps them to be comfortable IN the problem but does not solve it. Getting fathers the knowledge they need to turn back to, claim, and raise their children will solve the problem. Everyone knows the statistic of how child poverty increases dramatically when a dad is not in the home. Economic wealth has always been connected to family. The root cause of the myriad of issues plaguing our society originates from a single problem: young people not understanding who they are as a result of improper parenting.

Most single moms don't seem to know that a child's formative years are between the ages of 2 and 7. That is when a child forms or develops their adult personality. If a child is not instilled with the proper values, morals, and character development by age 7, it will be difficult for that child to be productive in society.

In order to be developed properly a child needs two parents. The word "parent" is comprised of the word "pare" and the suffix "ent". Pare means "to cut away the unwanted parts" and the suffix "ent" means "on the inside". So the word parent means to cut away the unwanted parts on the inside of a child. Once the unwanted parts are cut out of the child they must be replaced with strong morals and values. Parenting in this manner will lead a child to become productive. Now, the child is ready to be taught.

The most effective teaching tool a parent has at their disposal is "modeling". Children learn best from what they see their parent DO more than from what the children hear them say. Women can help future generations of women have better relationships by being a proper model for their children. The proper model for children is a married mom with a dad living in the home. This will allow them to SEE how to cultivate good relationships, how to deal with the opposite sex, and know that children are best raised in a two parent home.

GOD said it is not good that a man should be alone so he created woman. If a woman could raise a child alone GOD would have created her to conceive it alone. I understand that some men want to honor your mom for the work she did in raising you and your brothers. I feel the same way about my mom. However, we dishonor GOD in the process when we say that we are able to defy HIS order and do that which HE did not design us to do. GOD did not design or equip a woman to raise a boy into a man. If she could do it, GOD would have allowed Mary to raise Jesus as a single mother. A child (especially a boy) needs a man or a dad to lead him into manhood and into his GOD ordained destiny. A man was designed by GOD to organize a child and lead them into their destiny.

Relationships

A woman was designed to maintain that order.

Many men try to claim that their mother's raised them into manhood simply because they finished school and have a good job. However, there is a difference between worldly success and ordained destiny. A woman can lead a boy to stay out of trouble, finish school, find a job, and love his children. However, that is not the same as leading a boy to become a man or leading him into his GOD ordained destiny. Only a man can do that.

Men raised totally by women will always be missing something relative to the fullness of manhood unless they do something to fix it. Men raised by women MUST have their manhood fulfilled by spending considerable amounts of time around strong men. The thing that helped me was having strong male football coaches who were father figures and strong male military leaders.

They finished the job that my mother (whom I love so very dearly and appreciate greatly) was unequipped to do. It was other strong men that led me to understand the Bible and in how to allow the Holy Spirit to teach me. It was the Holy Spirit, who knows ALL things, who taught me to discover my GOD ordained destiny. Men who missed being raised by a man need the Holy Spirit to intervene and give them the knowledge they need to lead them to do that which GOD created them to do.

Every man must turn back and begin to properly parent and be a daddy for their own children. This is an absolute must. Don't worry about the relationship that you have with the children's mother. If there is not a court order to stay away, go back and get your children today. Women, it should not matter if he is with another woman or he still owes child support. Your child needs a daddy. Put your children, especially your sons, back under the authority and guidance of their father!

Now, some men are intimidated about raising their children because they don't really know what to do to properly love and raise a child. In order to get the knowledge you need, you must read. Please read my "Maximinzing Fatherhood". It contains everything a man needs to know on how to live his life, love his wife, and raise his children. You can read it, get all you need to know, and then you can stand before your family looking like a PRO. And no one will ever know that you didn't know.

Relationships

Chapter 11
HOW TO FIND A VIRTUOUS WOMAN

"The world and all things in it are valuable but the most valuable thing in the world is a virtuous woman." ~ Muhammad

A venerably wise person once asked the question "Who can find a virtuous woman because her price is far above rubies." The implication to the question is that a virtuous woman is hard to find because she is rare and that rarity gives her an expensive quality not found in most women. The word virtuous means one who possesses strength, power, and moral excellence, which lead to purpose, provision, protection, and peace. A virtuous woman is hard to find but a faithful man must do all that he can and spend all he has to find her. A faithful man must have a virtuous woman because just as every super woman needs a superman, every man who wants to be King needs a Coretta Scott.

The virtuous woman, like the faithful man, has characteristics and qualities that identify her as such. First and foremost she is trustworthy. The heart of her husband safely trusts in her, so that he will have no need of seducing other women. A virtuous woman will do good, not evil, to her husband all the days of her life. Whatever

Relationships

she wants in terms of clothing, jewelry, etc, she will work to get them on her own and may not necessarily depend on him to provide them. At the same time, a virtuous woman is a good home maker. When money is tight, for example, she can make a good meal out of seemingly nothing. She will even get up very early in the morning to prepare meals for her family as well as for those neighbors who might be needy.

A virtuous woman understands how to utilize her creative ability to earn the money to purchase a home and decorate it. She won't just give herself to any man to because she knows how to protect her virtue. She also exercises to take care of her body and keep herself healthy. A virtuous woman does not have low self-esteem, understands her personal value, and will retain her virtue in the light as well as the dark.

The reason the value of a virtuous woman is compared to the price of a ruby is because a good ruby is rare. A Star Ruby, in fact, is a very rare precious stone. When you look at it you will be able to clearly see that it has six perfect points of light but the six points of light that you see are only the end. There are also six perfect points at the beginning. Six plus six is twelve or the Bible number of "eternal perfection". A virtuous woman's beginning is perfect as well as her end just like the points of light in a Star Ruby. This accounts for the reason why her light shines brightly in the light as well as the dark. She retains her virtue during the day and she keeps her virtue at night.

The other thing about a virtuous woman is she works hard, extends herself to help the poor, and is never worried about her children being without provision. The clothing she wears is loose fitting, not tight, and the material and colors resemble that which a queen would wear. As a result of the way the virtuous woman carries herself in public, her husband is known and respected throughout in their city and is counted and consulted as a wise man among the city leaders.

The average woman of virtue is enterprising and knows how to bring wealth to her household. She keeps herself busy with the business affairs of her husband, in charitable causes, and the care of her home. The words of her mouth are full of wisdom, grace, and compassion. Therefore, her children call her blessed and her husband also praises her. Many women have learned to act virtuous and get treated as such but a true woman of virtue out shines them all. The favor that some women receive because of their external beauty can make a woman appear to be virtuous when she actually is not. The way that a man can discern a woman of true virtue is to give her something to do. The works of her hands will reveal whether she has the favor of GOD or not. The virtuous woman possesses strength, power, and moral excellence. Therefore, a true woman of virtue will always be rewarded with riches, honor, and glory.

Relationships

Every woman should strive to be a woman of virtue. Every woman should receive the same honor, glory and respect. The thing that most women must learn about men is that every man wants a virtuous woman. However, he will sleep with a bunch of women who will allow him to until he finds the one with true virtue. Women who only pretend to be virtuous will just get used by an unfaithful man until he finds the one who he really believes is the right one. Then they will just get left.

When a woman sees herself as something of value she will retain her virtue. She won't let anybody touch her or handle her who is not her husband. Retaining her virtue will make the men that she allows in her life see her as special or valuable. Men never put value on anything they have no knowledge of or can just use for sex. Rather than having sex virtuous women lead the men they are interested in into intimate conversation. Virtuous women want to talk to a man to discover what is in his mind. Women who have sex with a man too quickly never get to intimacy. Once she has sex with a man, he will feel like he doesn't have to talk anymore until he wants more sex. A man has to be made to recognize that a woman has value before they have sex. If he really recognizes her value, he will treat her like she is special and not lead her into sex until they are married. He will make sure that he captures the heart of her mind before another man asks for her hand.

Like any other hot commodity on the market, ladies, your value has nothing to do with what it cost to create you. Your value has to do with what another person is willing to sacrifice to marry you. It may have cost only $10 in canvass and paint to create the Mona Lisa but it is worth 700 million because someone is willing to sacrifice millions to get her. The water and dirt required to assemble your body may only cost $7. However, your price becomes far above rubies because that is the price the faithful man who recognizes your value would be willing to pay. Price is never an issue when a quality product is being presented. Jesus was willing to sacrifice His life to redeem you, so you need a husband who is willing to sacrifice all of his possessions and part of his life to be a part of yours.

A man who recognizes that a woman is valuable will understand that she is also value able. That is, she has the inherent gift, talent or ability to add to or increase his value. Once he has appraised her value, if he is a really sharp businessman, he will immediately move to appreciate it. To appreciate means to increase in value. In other words, he will want to show her that in return for adding value to him, he will add value to her. He will try to do something for her or offer her a proposal which leads her to see that partnering with him will be beneficial to her as well.

The faithful man will recognize a virtuous woman

immediately. He already understands that a real king is recognized by his crown. GOD created the woman to be like the crown of a king. A faithful man understands this and will be willing to place her in a prominent position to cover and protect his head. GOD made the woman to dress and adorn the man like a crown; to make him feel better and look stronger.

A crown is supposed to be positioned to protect the man's head and should be adorned with his finest jewels. A woman should not have anything to do with a man, then, who is not willing to place her in a prominent position in his life and who is unwilling to adorn her with his finest jewels.

The thing that makes a king different from an ordinary man is his crown. The thing that makes a great man different from an ordinary man is a virtuous woman. Just as a good crown protects a man's head, a good woman protects her man. She brings honor to him by exemplifying the crowning qualities of womanhood which are: a devotional spirit, modesty, liberality, wisdom, and virtue.

They say that behind every great man is a good woman. Examining the great men of history and the woman in their lives will reveal that this is true. No ordinary man could ever become great without the help of a good woman. GOD created virtuous women for the purpose of helping good men become great.

Barack Obama shared an interesting story that illustrates this point. He said that he and Michelle were stopped at a gas station just after he announced that we was going to run for President and he noticed the gas station attendant was her old boy friend. He said he told Michelle who the guy was and she got out of the car to speak to him.

It was then that he noticed that not only was the old boy friend working in a gas station, he was also looking kind of worn and dusty. So he stuck out his chest and started feeling good about himself. After the man had pumped the gas and walked away he told Michelle: "See, if you had married him instead of me, you wouldn't be married to the man running for President now." He said she lovingly straightened his tie and said, "If I were married to him, he would be running for President now." You see, a good woman can help her man achieve great things. Also, any great man will tell you that you cannot achieve greatness without having first experienced humility. A virtuous woman has a lovely way of keeping a great man humble.

THE TRUTH ABOUT SUBMISSION

Many good men have ruined and missed the opportunity to access the power of virtuous women because they tried to follow the false religious doctrine of submission. The manufacturer of the universe left us a book designed to be operating instructions for our

Relationships

lives. Misinterpretation of these operating instructions as a result of evil influence has caused a deep rift in male/female relationships. There is a Bible paragraph that reads "Wives submit yourselves unto your own husbands as unto the Lord (Ephesians 5:22)." This instruction was taken out of context and used to try to subordinate women to men. However, just before that paragraph a balancing instruction was given that is wholly ignored: "Submitting yourselves one to another in the fear of GOD (Ephesians 5:21)." Reading these instructions together shows us what GOD truly intended which is both the man and woman are to submit to each other, not just her to him. This is critical for men to understand because he actually needs a virtuous wife in order to be successful in life more than she needs him.

GOD put the man and woman together to add strength and power to one another. The wife was given as provision (pro = for; vision) to help her husband complete or fulfill the vision or mission he has established for their family. The Bible describes the wife as a help meet (a suitable, proper or fit helper) or someone who was created to help another complete their mission. A man must have a wife with gifts, talent, and abilities that complement his to assist him in completing his mission. A wife, in effect, carries the equipment that a man needs to achieve success.

Any woman can be a good mate for a man but a man needs a wife who is meet or suitable, proper, and fit for him if he is to complete what he has determined to do. A mate could help a man get along in life, but a meet will help him get ahead! A man can become rich with a mate but he will be wealthy with a meet. The family is the primary organization designed by GOD for wealth generation. A couple who is meet for each other are more likely to achieve victory and become wealthy!

It is very important, then, for a man who seeks wealth to understand that the Bible instructs men to submit to their wives. Most men will resist submitting to their wives for fear that it will make them look henpecked. However, there is nothing wrong with being henpecked when you are pecked by a good hen! Every man who wants to be King needs a Coretta Scott. Every superman needs a super woman. Being submitted to one another is critical if a marital union is going to work as well as create wealth. He submits to her, she submits to him; she has his back, he has her back; he supports her, she supports him. They work together to strengthen and empower each other.

Now, if a husband wants his wife to submit to him, he has to submit to her first. A leader always sets the example so he must always do for his wife first whatever he expects her to do for him. A leader never asks anyone to do anything that they are unwilling or have not already done themselves.

Relationships

When a couple is in complete submission, the two of them are submitted to each other in a way that neither of them is superior to the other. The Real Housewives of Atlanta's Ed and Lisa is the perfect example of a couple in that is submitted to one another. He is in submission to her and she is in submission to him; he supports her and she supports him.

To be clear just so that we don't misunderstand due to different understandings of a word's meaning, the word submission is a combination of the prefix "sub" and the base word "mission". Sub simply means to be under, support, or hold up like a sub-floor. To be in submission means to hold up, to support another in a mission, or to get under one's mission. A husband must hold up or support his wife in the pursuit of her goals, aspirations, and ambitions and she must hold up or support her him in his.

Genesis 2:22 describes the woman being built from the man's rib. The word rib is translated from the Hebrew word "tsal'ah" which means a curved pillar, timber, or beam. A wife was designed to be a natural means of support and strength to her husband; to lift or hold him up. This is the reason 1 Corinthians 11:8-9 says that man was not created for the woman but the woman was created for the man. The truth that is quietly being revealed here is the man needs help. The woman doesn't really need help, but he does! It is nice whenever a woman gets help or support from her husband but she really doesn't need it.

Most of the problems that men and women have in submitting to one another are due to the confusion over what the word submit really means. When the word submission is used in the context of male/female relationships most women hear the word subjection. The word subjection is comprised of the prefix "sub" and the base word "ject", meaning to throw and "ion" which means an act or process. To be in subjection in this context is an act or process of being thrown or throwing one's self under another to be walked on. However, the word subject also means one who is submitted to or under the guidance and direction of another.

A wife must be subject to her husband in terms of being amenable to his guidance and direction. But she must never allow herself to become subject to him in terms of being walked on. The same is true for a man. He must submit himself to his wife as his queen. However, he must never become her subject.

Relationships

Chapter 12
LOVE'S FINANICAL RISKS AND REWARDS

"Fear cannot be without some hope nor hope without some fear." ~ Baruch Spinoza

I have heard ladies joking that the next time they plan to get married they are going to do a credit check on their man first. It sounded funny each time I heard it but then I thought, hey that is a good idea. The reason it's a good idea is because a person's credit history can tell you a great deal about their character and whether or not they are trustworthy.

When we apply for credit, we give the creditor our word that we will repay them so much per month over a certain period of time. Once we give them our word they require us to sign our name. A credit history report is really a summary of whether or not you keep your word and whether or not your name is good. If you do not keep your word, they place a comment under your name on your credit or credibility report that alerts the next creditor that your name is no good because your word can not be trusted.

Relationships

Once a woman marries a man she takes his name. If the man has a poor credit history, her name will be forever associated with his name. If his credit was no good, now her credibility will be suspect. When making an omelet, two eggs are mixed together and become one. There is no way to tell where one egg ends and the other egg begins. No matter how good your egg is, when it is mixed with a rotten egg the whole omelet will stink. Therefore, women must take a critical look at a man's credit because she will be taking on his name and the credibility associated with that name. It might not be a bad idea, then, when a man asks to marry you to tie your answer to a review of his TRW.

On the other hand, because a woman was designed by GOD to be a man's helper, men must take an especially critical look at a woman's employment record or resume to discover whether or not she has the ability to work with him properly. A man who wants to be wealthy will need a woman to work with to achieve that goal successfully. Therefore, he must apply the same processes that Human Resource Managers use to qualify potential employees. A woman's resume will tell you a lot about her ability to serve, how she will perform, and whether she can commit to long term relationships.

If a woman's resume shows that she has a pattern of quitting or being fired after short periods of time, it indicates that she will have difficulty building a long term relationship. When the going gets tough, she will get going. The area on a resume that gives employers great insight into this aspect of a person's life is the references section. The length of time that a woman has known or had a relationship with her references is a good indicator of how long she will be able to maintain a relationship with you.

If the performance area of her resume does not show that she is innovative, it means that she is not creative. She is the type of employee that must be supervised closely in order to gain a minimum amount of productivity. Although a woman may be very nice, attractive and sexy, a wife that must be monitored or supervised closely is a liability rather than an asset.

The other tool employers use to determine if a person will be suitable, proper, and fit for the position or a perfect match for a particular position is the job application. The things that a woman does in her spare time, under her list of hobbies, and how she serves others as a volunteer gives an employer an idea of how she will serve as an employee. Those areas also provide great insight into her inherent gifts, talents, and abilities. Men, a wife is a valuable asset that must be employed to do a very important job within your marriage. Therefore, when you are looking for someone to marry, you must learn how to skillfully conduct a job interview.

Relationships

Marriage is Business

Most people view marriage as an agreement to love, honor, and cherish another for the rest of their lives but that is only one side of the equation. When a man asks a woman to marry him it is said that he "proposes" to her. A "proposal" is a business plan that establishes how one intends to assist others in conducting or advancing their business. Every single person has an personal responsibility to handle or conduct business affairs on their own behalf. A man who proposes marriage is simply offering to merge their individual business affairs together. In doing so, he must lead his potential bride to be to see how she will benefit from their marriage personally and financially. Marriage is not just a social contract it also a business arrangement wherein two individuals become a corporation. All of your business affairs will be incorporated together. When either one of you want to purchase or liquidate the major assets of your corporation, you will need the cooperation of your spouse.

Recognizing now that every marriage is a business, we must realize that every viable business must have a vision, mission and a financial plan detailing how the business with acquire and disburse its funds. The principal owners of the business must already have a vision, established the mission, and developed their financial plan before forming the corporation. However, most couples spend too much time planning their wedding rather than planning their marriage or business operation. Therefore, they either never develop the plan before hand or they try to formulate it after uncoordinated spending has created a crisis. Bad financial management is the leading cause of both business failure and divorce in America. It would be wise, then, for couples who are preparing to spend their lives together to plan how they will spend their money before they get married.

The two main financial benefits of marriage are division of labor and economy of scale. Single people have to do all the domestic labor and pay all of the bills alone. Married couples can split the chores and split the bills. Once two single people become married the housework will take half the time and it will only cost half as much to live because two can live cheaper than one. The time and money saved can be invested to make more money. The enterprising couple can use the extra money and time to build a business and create an independent or secondary income stream. Less enterprising couples can use the extra money to pay down their mortgage or pad their retirement. They can use the extra time to make more money by working a second job.

Women Make Men Wealthy

Each person was born with inherent knowledge, gift, talent, and ability that if mined and marketed properly, someone would pay you for handsomely. Your spouse can be your passport to financial success if you understand how to market and manage their assets to formulate a business. Individuals can get rich but strong committed partners working together can create wealth. Family is the primary organization for wealth generation. Every family can be wealthy. You can get my CD "Money Does Grow on Trees" to see how this works for a family or my other CD "Surprising Secrets of the Fortune 500" to see how it works for business. There are universal principles that, when applied properly, are designed to create wealth naturally. The principles will work for everyone who puts them to work.

Now, every woman was born with the gift of service inside of her. She was designed by GOD to be a helper to her husband. The husband must recognize, then, that GOD made her to help him and learn how to utilize her gift. 1 Corinthians 11:8-9 says "…the man is not of the woman; but the woman is of the man. Neither was the man created for the woman; but the woman is for the man." You see, a woman was created for the man to be his helper but here's the key point: GOD did not create him for her, GOD made her for him. GOD looked at Adam and concluded: that brother needs help! The woman does not really need a helper but the man does! Therefore a husband must find a way to utilize his wife's gift, along with her talent and abilities, to help him create a strong family and build wealth. If he understands how to do this, she can make it happen!

Mommy gives birth to everything essential in a marriage but it is daddy that determines destiny. Whether a family becomes strong or grows to become wealthy will depend on whether or not the husband or father cultivates his family member's gifts, provides proper care, and creates the proper environment for productivity. Men can create and control the environment of their homes through their words. If we understand how to talk to or teach and train our family members, we can lead them to recognize who GOD created them to be. Once they realize who they are, we can put them to proper use within the family in a way that will increase their personal sense of value. They will then begin to add value by becoming a productive resource. A man will then be able to tap into the treasure that GOD placed inside of them to bring prosperity to his family. Becoming a source of value allows us to move our family from poverty to prosperity through the knowledge, gifts, talents, and abilities that GOD placed inside of us.

Most men are operating at a financial deficit because no one ever shared this information with us before. The reason the average man doesn't understand how to utilize women is because Adam was asleep when GOD made Eve. Thus, most men have no clue about how a woman was built or what she was created to do. The reason the average man experiences shortfalls financially, then, is because no one ever taught him that a wife is the most valuable asset on the planet. Consequently, a wife is also the most undervalued and underutilized asset on the planet.

Any man who recognizes how to identify the knowledge, gifts, talents, and abilities inside of his wife and realizes how to utilize those assets to bring his family's vision to fruition, he will have wealth and prosperity well beyond his imagination. GOD gave a man the woman to help him prosper. If a husband lets his wife do what GOD created her to do, and not try to keep her down to a degree so he can feel dominant in the relationship, she will use her gift, talent and ability to virtually spin straw into gold. The power that GOD placed in her will cause this to happen.

It is in a woman's nature to help a man. If her husband does not give her something to help him with, she will look to help someone else. She will not submit to him if he has not given her anything to submit to. I shared earlier that the word sub means under or support. The word submission, then, means to provide support or to get under one's mission. If a man does not give a woman a mission to support, there is no reason for her to give him submission. This is the reason why it appears that a woman is more apt to submit to her pastor or her boss before she will submit her husband. The difference between him and them is they give her a vision or mission to support. The boss and the preacher will let her help them but her husband won't. Husbands who do not give their wives anything substantial to do other than housework often feel they are not being catered to. They complain that their wives won't serve them so they divorce their wife and marry their secretary.

Divorce Can Be Financial Death

Divorce usually comes to a marriage when the couple is on a divided course; she wants to go in one direction and he wants to go in another. Divorce is one of the leading causes of poverty for women and children in America. Divorce can turn a rich man to ruin almost overnight. This is the reason wealthy people do not divorce. Wealthy women will remain with their cheating husbands to protect the wealth and inheritance of their children. Wealthy people understand the benefits of marriage. Therefore, they refuse to forfeit those benefits and they refuse to take any action that could place their children in poverty.

The bible says that GOD hates divorce. Women who are wealthy know that divorce is not wise because it is a violation of GOD's word. This is the reason why the bible describes wisdom as a woman who will consistently do what GOD said. A man who has a woman of wisdom will have wealth. A woman of wisdom will not condemn her children to poverty and possibly miss her chance to live in eternity. As stated in a previous chapter, refusing to forgive can be costly financially. This is the reason why wealthy women will stand by their cheating man when middle class and poor women won't. They stand by their husband in an effort to keep their children out of poverty.

Many couples divorce after the children grow up and leave home. This is called the "Empty Nest Syndrome". The Empty Nest Syndrome affects couples who spent too much time majoring in the minors and forgot to make a plan for their marriage after the minors were gone. Childless couples begin to go their separate ways or do things apart because the activities they normally did together centered around the children. The word divorce comes from the word "divert" which means to set on opposite or diverging courses. A couple that is divorced or on their way to becoming divorced are no longer "going together". They are therefore setting themselves out on different courses. Divorce usually comes after a period of time where couples stop communicating or having conversations. It is critical then to marriage survival for a couple to continually talk about and look forward to what they plan to do together after the children leave home.

The word conversation means the process of causing conversion. The purpose of conversation in the later stages of marriage is simply to cause conversion from thinking like parents to thinking and planning like a childless couple. The objective is to produce a meeting of the minds so that they are both thinking alike. Some people refer to being in a relationship as "talking to" another person. Couples who talk to each other frequently are in the process of causing their minds to convert, to meet or come into agreement. Those couples who will have an empty nest in a few years must begin having conversations that causes them to plan how they will convert or change the way they are living and the things they will do. Some couples will plan to sell the larger home for a smaller one or to move from one district that had higher property taxes due to better schools to one with lower taxes. Others plan to travel to all the places they couldn't go with all of the children in tow.

Sometimes the only reason a couple remained together was for the children.If they recognize that they cannot come into agreement or if one or both refuses to convert, that is when these couples usually separate or divorce. When couples stop meeting together at the heart or remaining one in their minds, they begin to decline in economic power and start to lose the financial benefits of marriage. Divided marriage means divided money and divided money leads to poverty. Sadly, couples who spent 3 or 4 decades together can end up living separately in poverty on their individual social security.

Some couples stay together because they can't afford to live apart. The debt they are carrying compared to the money they having coming in locks them in marital captivity. When women didn't work outside of the home their mothers would advise them to put away some of the "butter and egg" money they would get from their husbands so they could afford to leave if they had too. It is wise today for each individual in a married couple to have "mad money". That's in the event one gets mad and needs to have another place to stay for a few days.

Good Marriage Management Leads To Wealth

Divorce often arises due to bad marriage leadership and bad marriage management. Men have the responsibility to lead and women have a duty to manage a marriage. The leader however also has a duty to monitor the manager. The wife may have control over the check book but the husband must conduct a quarterly audit. The wife may have a duty to see that all the bills are paid but the husband must check periodically to see that they are paid and paid on time. Just like every powerful nation each strong family must have a check and balance system. If the husband trusts his wife to handle managing the family's finances, his wife should not have a problem if he wants to audit their system to make sure it is working.

It is always best for one person, whoever is best at doing it, to manage the family's money. Uncoordinated spending can reek havoc on the family finances when two people are writing checks or making withdrawals without the one being aware of what the other is doing. The other person must make sure the managing partner can account for their transactions. Again, the non-managing partner must make sure the managing partner can account for all of their actions and the money is being managed properly.

You don't want to wake up and realize the managing partner has been buying a ton of stuff with cash and on credit while floating the bills. For one person the word DEBT is an acronym that means Don't Ever Buy on Time. But to the other it may mean Doesn't Everybody Buy on Time? Sometimes people use credit cards like it is free money and can quickly saddle a family with a lot of debt. Therefore, each couple must be able to check their spouse's spending to make sure the family doesn't become overwhelmed with debt.

I have seen couples spiral into financial trouble when they stop talking to each other. When couples stop talking after awhile they stop touching. A lack of talking and touching leads eventually to a halt in sexual intimacy. People often substitute a loss of sexual intimacy with other things. Some substitute sex with food while some turn to gambling and others will substitute shopping for sex. Whatever the substitute for some reason it always turns to excess. Those using food to comfort themselves often balloon in weight to the point that it affects their health. Gambling for many people becomes obsessive to the point where they can't make themselves stop. Shopping for others becomes addictive and the person starts to make themselves believe that spending is a form of saving. Buying a $100 item that they absolutely did not need at 20% off is saving $20. Continually talking and touching keeps a couple meeting at the minds and makes it easier to manage the money in a marriage.

Relationships

Daddy Determines Financial Destiny

The success of a family financially relies heavily on the man or husband achieving victory over himself. A man who is cheating, according to an article in Men's Health Magazine, spends about $10,000 annually on the activity. That money is diverted from investment and other activities that could have moved the family forward financially. Therefore, to overcome his cheating ways or to avoid becoming a cheater, a man must become completely developed spiritually.

Growing into spiritual maturity is necessary in order for a man to lead his family to reach its destiny. In order for his family to overcome the pressures and distractions of the world which lead them to take actions that can cause financial ruin, a man must become whole within himself and connected and one with GOD. When the husband and father has become who GOD created him to be, the other members of the family will be more likely to come to know who they are, how they are supposed to behave, and what they were assigned by GOD to do. If the husband has become a regenerated man, his family will be able to become whatever he or she was created to become. Whatever that particular family was designed by GOD to be will be impacted by how far the father was able to travel on the path of righteousness.

When men have not come to be whom GOD created

them to be, it is impossible to lead their family to become what GOD created it to be. A man must already be what he is trying to lead his family to become. A family that is moving steadily toward reaching their destiny always proper financially. Families that are not moving toward their destiny get pulled down financially. These truisms are based on a universal principle like the law of gravity. Airplanes fly because the power of lift and thrust supersede the law of gravity. Therefore, families that are thrusting toward their destiny always get a lift financially.

Freedom From Debt Leads To Financial Success

The process for achieving eternal bliss in a marriage depends largely on whether or not the family has achieved financial success. Financial success relies heavily on the couple being one in heart, mind, and spirit. The quicker they get to that point, which is the point of being married, the less it will cost them in terms of financial stress. It is critical for a couple to move far away from their single life as quickly as possible. The place where couples make the biggest mistake is trying to be married while still living in the home they lived in when they were single.

Living in the home of a single person keeps you connected to the life of a single person. Couples who were "shacking-up" or living together prior to marriage have the greatest difficulty remaining married because

Relationships

they get married and try to live in the same house that they did while single. There is a spiritual tie that binds us to every level of development in life. The connection to that level involves an attachment to the people, places, activities, and things that we encounter at that level. In order to move up to the next level we must break our attachment to some of those people, places, activities and things. A home is one of those things. If a couple wants to quickly achieve wedded bliss and reduce the financial risk of divorce, they must begin their marriage in a newly acquired home rather than one that either of them owned prior to marriage. The process of becoming married is tough. When one still lives in the home that they lived in while they were single during this process makes it harder for them to become married and easier to retreat back to being single again when times get tough. A couple can do themselves a big favor financially by selling the homes they owned individually and begin their marriage in a home that they own jointly.

Single people who are planning or hope to be married one day that own a home must make preparations financially to be married. They must first consolidate all of their credit card, student loan, and other debt by taking out a second mortgage on their home. Second, they must take ALL of the money that would have been used to make monthly payments on those debts and use it to rapidly reduce the amount they owe on the mortgage. There are mortgage reduction strategies that will allow you to pay off your mortgage several years early well as reduce the amount of interest you would have had to pay over life of loan. You can straight to the point books containing these strategies on my website at WealthBuilderSeminars.com. Following these strategies will help a single person prepare to be married financially and will reduce the amount of debt that they bring into a marriage.

Single persons who do not own a home must also prepare financially to be married by quickly reducing the amount of debt they are carrying. When two people who are both saddled with a lot of debt get married it often becomes a financial weight that is too heavy for the couple to carry. Therefore, those who are planning to be married must begin to apply tried and true rapid debt reduction strategies. These strategies, when applied consistently, will not only reduce your debt quickly but will also lead to total debt freedom. You can get a book "13 Steps to Debt Freedom" on my website at WealthBuilderSeminars.com. If you diligently apply these strategies, you will soon be debt free.

The Financial Risk of Adoption

Men, this next point is going to make some women mad at me. However, I must retain my integrity by addressing every issue equally even if it makes one side unhappy. So we are going to just pretend that they can't hear us having this conversation. Now, to be fair, this situation could happen to a woman also but that occurrence is very rare. However, a man who marries a woman that already has children must wait until he is absolutely certain that he will remain married before he commits the honorable act of adopting her children. Once he adopts her children they become his children. It does not matter to the law and the courts who actually fathered the children at that point, they become his. If he divorces the mother, he cannot divorce the children. Ergo, he will be financially responsible for them into early adulthood. Most women in this situation, once divorced, demand that he pay support for them. There are some who never pursued the biological father for support that will hound the adoptive father for support in court and repeatedly return to court for support increases. Marriage is already a great financial risk for single successful men with no children. But if a divorce occurs and children are involved, the woman could walk away with all of her assets and half of his. I am not advising against adopting the children. A family blends better when they all have the same name. People who are called the same thing, like a sports team, often work better together as a group. I am advising that a man take careful consideration about the life and health of his marriage before he makes that move.

Every Family Can Be Wealthy

Every person in a family has within them inherent

knowledge, gifts, talents, abilities and energy. Each day, most of us, lease our knowledge, gifts, talents, abilities and energy to an employer for small sums of money, which the employer uses to make large sums of money. According to The US Department of Commerce, the US auto industry makes $14 for every $1 that it pays it workers. The worker who earns $28 per hour earns their employer $3,136 per day. What if you could find a way to keep the lion's share of the value of what your knowledge, gifts, talents, abilities and energy are really worth for you and your family? You could potentially become as wealthy as Ford or GM. Once a family changes the way that they utilize their knowledge, gifts, talents, abilities and energy, they will be able to change their position financially.

Relationships

ABOUT THE AUTHOR

Dr William "Dr Will" Small holds a PhD in Biblical Studies and has over 40 years experience conducting personal, professional, and family counseling. Dr Will is an award winning presenter of Domestic Violence Prevention and Awareness seminars. And he is an Association for Talent Development Master Trainer and Consultant. You can find out more about Dr Will by visiting his website at www.drwillenterprises.com.

RECOMMENDED READING

The following books are older works but they contain the best information on life, love and relationships that you will ever find. The best works and the best wines are always vintaged:

- Maximizing Fatherood – Dr William Small
- Single Mothers and Sons – Dr William Small
- Money Does Grow On Trees - Dr William Small
- The 7 Habits of Highly Effective People – Stephen Covey
- The 8th Habit - Stephen Covey
- Awaken the Giant Within – Anthony Robbins
- Change Your Thoughts, Change Your Life - Wayne W. Dyer
- Click: Ten Truths for Relationships – George Fraser
- Goals: Setting and Achieving Them on Schedule – Zig Ziglar
- How to Be Wanted - Romy Miller

  How to Win Friends and Influence People – Dale Carnegie

Relationships

- If I'm So Wonderful, Why Am I Still Single - Susan Page
- Is It Love or Is It Sex - Carla Wills-Brandon
- Live Your Dreams - Les Brown
- The Master Key System - Charles F. Haanel
- Psycho-Cybernetics - Maxwell Maltz
- The Secret – Rhonda Byrne
- The Success Principles - Jack Canfield/Janet Switzer
- Think and Grow Rich – Napoleon Hill
- When Good People Have Affairs - Mira Kirshenbaum
- Why Mr. Right Can't Find You - J. M. Kearns
- Women Have All the Power - Chandra Taylor

Dr William Small

Relationships